THINKING MATHEMATICALLY

INTEGRATING ARITHMETIC AND ALGEBRA IN ELEMENTARY SCHOOL

THOMAS P. CARPENTER

MEGAN LOEF FRANKE

LINDA LEVI

HEINEMANN • PORTSMOUTH, NH

Heinemann
A division of Reed Elsevier Inc.
361 Hanover Street
Portsmouth, NH 03801–3912
www.heinemann.com

Offices and agents throughout the world

The development of this program was supported in part by a grant from the National Science Foundation (ESI9911679). It is based in part on research supported by the Department of Education, Office of Educational Research and Improvement to the National Center for Improving Student Learning and Achievement in Mathematics and Science (R305A60007-98). The opinions expressed in this book do not necessarily reflect the position, policy, or endorsement of the National Science Foundation, the Department of Education, OERI, or the National Center.

Library of Congress Cataloging-in-Publication Data
Carpenter, Thomas P.
Thinking mathematically : integrating arithmetic and algebra in elementary school / Thomas P.
  Carpenter, Megan Loef Franke, Linda Levi.
     p. cm.
    Includes bibliographical references and index. Developing mathematical thinking—Equality—Developing and using relational thinking—Making conjectures about mathematics—Equations with multiple variables and repeated variables—Representing conjectures symbolically—Justification and proof—Ordering multiple operations—"If . . . then . . ." statements : relations involving addition, subtraction, multiplication, division, and equality—Conclusion.
    ISBN 0-325-00565-6
    1. Arithmetic—Study and teaching (Elementary).   2. Algebra—Study and teaching (Elementary).   I. Franke, Megan Loef.   II. Levi, Linda.   III. Title.
  QA135.6 .C37   2003
  372.7'2—dc21   2002014184

Editor: Victoria Merecki
Production: Elizabeth Valway
Cover design: Joni Doherty
Typesetter: Argosy Publishing
Photography: Paul Baker
CD-ROM development: Enrique Rueda, Tracy Madison, and Joe Lucero
Manufacturing: Steve Bernier

Printed in the United States of America on acid-free paper
09 08   VP   9 10

We dedicate this book to Bob Davis.
Without his pioneering work,
it would not have been possible.

CONTENTS

 This icon appears when there are video episodes on the CD illustrating the ideas in the text.

FOREWORD

A third-grade class is discussing the conjecture that an odd number plus an odd number equals an even number. Does this work for all numbers? The students are busily at work, producing long lists of examples: $7 + 9 = 16$, $9 + 11 = 20$; $101 + 213 = 314$. All of a sudden, a problem emerges: Sheena and Jeannie announce that they can prove that the conjecture cannot be proved. Why? "Because numbers go on and on forever, and that means odd numbers and even numbers go on forever, so you cannot prove that Betsy's conjecture always works." The class is thrown into crisis: what does this imply for all the ideas that they have already accepted? After all, nothing else that they think they know has been tested with *all* numbers. A classmate presses:

Mei: [*Pointing at posted conjectures*] Then why don't you say that *those* conjectures are not always true? Why do you say that *those* are true, because we haven't tried every number that there was, so you can't really say that *those* are true if you're saying that you want to try every number there ever was.

Jeannie: I never *said* that they were true all the time . . .

Mei: Then why do, then why didn't you disagree when like Liz and everybody agreed with those conjectures?

Jeannie: Because I wasn't *thinking* about it.

What is going on in this little moment of epiphany? Three things, not equally evident. First is a glimpse of the profound mathematical thinking of which ordinary children are capable. Second is a view of the remarkable terrain of human endeavor that we call mathematics. And, third, least apparent, is the complex work of teaching needed to bring the first (students' capacity for mathematical ideas and thinking) into productive contact with the second (the rich and wonderful territory of mathematics).

Thinking Mathematically offers the reader a voyage into these three intertwined elements of children's mathematics education, focusing on the interface between arithmetic and algebra. As the authors note, mathematics involves ways of thinking, including ways to generate ideas, express and represent them, and justify that they are true. Moreover, "elementary school children are capable of learning how to engage in this type of thinking in mathematics, but often they are not given the opportunity to do so." We agree. But what constitutes such *opportunity*? The authors have woven a text with the resources for answering that question. What would it take for elementary students to be engaged not only in learning the powerful ideas of the subject but also its essential questions, and ways of thinking about those questions?

First, Carpenter, Franke, and Levi help us see that one thing that is required is a perspective on mathematics as a domain of reasoning about objects and their relations, that mathematical work involves seeking, examining, and naming patterns, and investigating the truth of claims about those objects, relations, and patterns. A central notion here is that of *conjecture*, or claims that seem plausible but which are not yet established. The book is filled with examples of conjectures that contribute to fundamental ideas of elementary arithmetic, such as:

1. When you add a number to another number and then you subtract the number you added, you get the number you started with.
2. When you add an odd number to another odd number, the answer is an even number.

These conjectures, with their sweeping generality, demand careful inspection in order to determine if they seem plausible, or if holes are visible when examined at close range. Expressing them clearly helps. For example, writing the first conjecture as $a + b - b = a$ makes its structure clearer and, hence, easier to analyze. The power of symbolic notation is evident when all those words can be condensed to this elegantly compressed expression.

Representing the second conjecture pictorially can provide a transparent proof of the claim:

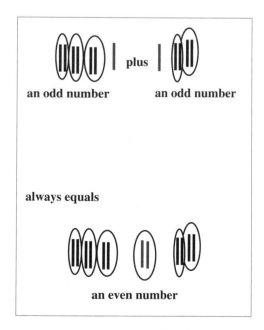

Knowing that the definition of an odd number is a number that, when grouped in twos, leaves a remainder of one, permits this diagram, and then the proof that the claim is true. This could also be represented compactly as

Through processes of mathematical reasoning, established patterns and ideas are developed into new ones. This generation of new ideas, then representing, and then investigating them is the perspective on elementary arithmetic that these authors provide: it is a rich portrait of that arithmetic set in a broader perspective on mathematics, and on what it means to do and learn it. And having this perspective is one step toward building opportunities for students.

Second, *opportunity* to engage in that mathematics depends on how it is framed and developed in classrooms. Central are the tasks that teachers proffer and what they do to scaffold them. Carpenter, Franke, and Levi offer resources for this crucial link between mathematical studies and the minds of young children. And their tastes in problems are broad: we find puzzles, situated word problems, and abstract investigations in the boundary domain between arithmetic and algebra. Each example develops the reader's sensibilities—as well as repertoire—for good mathematical questions and problems. They are good because they have mathematical weight and because they generate new questions and ideas. They are also good because they can be made accessible to elementary children, thereby pulling them into encounters with challenging, generative, and fascinating kinds of mathematical work.

Opportunity also rests, third, with what students themselves are helped to produce. Students' own ideas are resources for their own and others' learning. Their representations stimulate others' thinking, and their explanations challenge and extend. Too often we hear said about a group of children, "Our students cannot do this sort of work," but the speaker is forgetting that "this sort of work," this mathematical thinking in arithmetic and algebra—as in our earlier example—is something that *must* be learned. Hence, it must be taught. The book overflows with supports for the mathematical work of the teacher in pressing students, provoking, supporting, pointing, and attending with care. Specific ideas are offered—moves to try, examples to offer, questions to produce.

But ensuring that the sort of *opportunity* that this book envisions for elementary students to engage in serious and significant mathematical thinking depends on more than a perspective on mathematics, a view of children as capable, and a rich set of resources for bridging students with mathematics. It depends on teachers who can hear the mathematics in students' talk, who can shape and offer problems of an adequate size and sufficient scope, and who can steer such problems to a productive point. Like their students, teachers need opportunities to learn. This book provides such opportunities, from the mathematics problems for teachers that tie up each chapter, to the detailed portraits of tasks and of students' work with those problems. These resources can offer teachers, individually and collaboratively, material for the study of teaching and of mathematics.

Hyman Bass and Deborah Loewenberg Ball

ACKNOWLEDGMENTS

Many people have contributed to our understanding of children's mathematical thinking and to the work that has resulted in this book. We are constantly learning about children's mathematical thinking, and Victoria Jacobs has been crucial in helping us learn through her research on the effects of our professional development program, her probing questions, and her insight into how teachers and children learn.

We have been fortunate to work with a group of dedicated, intelligent colleagues at the University of Wisconsin-Madison, the University of California-Los Angeles, and San Diego State University. We could not have written this book without the many contributions of Jae-meen Baek, Daniel Battey, Patricia Berman, Victoria Deneroff, Julie Koehler, Margaret Pligge, Denise Raynes Pitcher, Toni Protti, and Joi Spencer.

We owe special thanks to the teachers who provided us an opportunity to learn about the development of algebraic thinking in their classrooms. We shared the excitement of learning together how children's mathematical thinking develops, and they provided invaluable insights in helping us to talk about what we were learning. We cannot possibly list all the teachers who have contributed to our understanding of children's thinking and the development of this book, but the following teachers contributed to this book over an extended period of time: Sue Berthouex, Mary Bostrom, Cathy Bullock, Karen DeCotis, Jessica Fairbanks, Karen Falkner, Susan Gehn, Janice Gratch, Linda Jaslow, Mazie Jenkins, Margaret Jensen, Annie Keith, Virginia Koberstein, Thad Loef, Dawn Eternick Michaels, Lilliam Paetzold, Julie Kern Schwerdtfeger, Kathleen Statz, Carrie Valentine, and Barbara Wiesner. JoAnn Isken, Linda McQuillen, and Mary Ramberg also contributed to the success of the project through their support of the teachers participating in this work.

Our advisory board—Deborah Ball, Hyman Bass, Elizabeth Fennema, James Kaput, Carolyn Kieran, Deborah Schifter—helped us understand what it means for children to think mathematically, and provided us with carefully considered, insightful reactions to earlier drafts of this book. We also thank Stephanie Biagetti, James Brickwedde, Roger Howe, Kenneth

Jewell, and Mary Lindquist for their invaluable feedback on the next to last draft of this book.

Joe Lucero and Tracy Madison brought both technical skill and an understanding of children to their videotaping of the children and classes for the CD that accompanies this book, and Enrique Rueda applied his exceptional understanding of multimedia technology to produce a CD that is the highlight of the book. Paul Baker demonstrated understanding and skill in taking the photographs for the book.

We also would like to thank Leigh Peake and Victoria Merecki for believing in the project and supporting us throughout the process of creating and publishing this book.

Finally we would like to thank all the children who were so patient in helping us understand their thinking. This is really their story, and we are indebted to them for helping us to tell it.

INTRODUCTION

For sixteen years we have been working with a group of elementary school teachers to study how children learn mathematics and mathematical ways of thinking. We have found that children have a great deal of informal knowledge about mathematics. In *Children's Mathematics*, we described how children's intuitive understandings about basic number concepts can provide a foundation upon which to build children's understanding of arithmetic concepts and skills. For the last five years we have been studying how to help children build on their emerging knowledge of arithmetic to provide a foundation for learning algebra.

We have found that children throughout the elementary grades are capable of learning powerful unifying ideas of mathematics that are the foundation of both arithmetic and algebra. Learning and articulating these ideas both enhances children's understanding of arithmetic and provides children with a solid basis for extending their knowledge of arithmetic to learn algebra. Making unifying ideas of mathematics a focus of discussion also addresses fundamental issues of equity. Here the ideas of all students can be drawn into the conversation so that students can all build on their mathematical understanding in ways that prepare them for future mathematical learning.

We, along with the teachers who have worked with us, are convinced that the perspective presented in this book represents a natural extension of the ideas in *Children's Mathematics*, one that takes conversations with children to the next level. It provides a framework for teachers and students to reflect on their implicit knowledge of arithmetic concepts and procedures, to ask questions about why we do things the way we do and how we know that we can do them that way.

As with *Children's Mathematics*, much of our emphasis in this book is on understanding children's mathematical thinking and the mathematics that is embedded in their thinking. We do not provide prescriptions for how to teach, but we do describe a number of types of problems and forms of questioning that we have found useful for eliciting children's thinking and for fostering growth in mathematical understanding. Our goal is to help you understand your own students' thinking so that you can help them make sense of the mathematics they are learning by building on their knowledge, skills, and problem-solving strategies.

In *Thinking Mathematically* we provide more extended examples of classroom dialogue than we did in *Children's Mathematics* to try to capture how ideas may emerge and illustrate the problems and questions that may help elicit them. Throughout the development of the ideas in this book, we have been fortunate to work with a number of teachers who are committed to understanding children's mathematical thinking, and we have included a number of Teacher Commentaries to capture their voices. One of the goals in including these teacher narratives is to portray the struggle that they have gone through and to emphasize that there are no easy answers. These teachers are saying: "This is what I did," not "This is the way you should do it."

Another unique feature of *Thinking Mathematically* is the collection of Challenges at the end of each chapter. The Challenges offer teachers a variety of opportunities to get involved with student thinking and the development of algebraic thinking. Some Challenges entail constructing problems to use with your students. Others involve trying out specific problems or activities with students or solving mathematical problems yourself. We designed the Challenges to support ongoing investigation of the ideas as one shares them with others, tests them out with students, and engages in making sense of the mathematics.

As was the case with *Children's Mathematics,* we have included on an accompanying CD examples of children's mathematical thinking. The examples include both extended interactions with individual children and classroom interactions. The examples are linked to specific narrative in the text, and an icon appears in the margin of the text to indicate the related episode on the CD. We recommend viewing the specific episodes on the CD when you read the related text, as the text provides some context for understanding the examples, and the examples on the CD provide rich illustrations of the ideas in the narrative. A reading of the text would not be complete without viewing the accompanying episodes.

Children's Mathematics focused on mathematical thinking in the early grades. *Thinking Mathematically* provides a basis for dialogue across all elementary grades. Although the numbers and contexts may be different, many of the underlying themes are appropriate for children from the primary grades through the middle grades. It takes a long time to develop deep understanding of fundamental mathematical ideas. We hope that *Thinking Mathematically* can provide a basis for teachers at all grades to work together to provide opportunities for students to develop that understanding.

TEACHER COMMENTARY I.1

My goal in teaching mathematics is to ensure that all children learn with understanding. I want all children to see the big ideas in mathematics. I think all children can learn with understanding. There are many children who have special needs. These children need more experiences with things that make sense and they need people to help them make connections so that they can see the big ideas in mathematics. Teaching with understanding builds on children's strengths. For many children, their weakness is learning procedures without understanding. These children will never get to understanding by practicing procedures they don't understand. What children learn today should help them the next day. For children who learn without seeing the big ideas, each day seems like a brand-new thing.

I recently interviewed ten fourth and fifth graders whose mathematics instruction had not focused on big ideas. These children all had been taught procedures that didn't make sense to them, so they didn't remember them. They often pieced together different algorithms in senseless ways. It was painful to watch them solve problems; I could have cried. They had no number sense. They didn't use relational thinking because they didn't even know that math is about relationships. When they were done, many students looked at me and asked, "Did I do it right?" Children who don't have an understanding have to look to the outside for validation. They don't look inside and think, I know I did it right. Unless someone teaches them how to learn mathematics with understanding, they will be lost. That cycle of failure will just continue. I don't want to see that with children.

Yesterday I was working with a child who was solving the multiplication problem 129×18. She was using the distributive property in several ways. When she was done, I asked her why she solved the problem that way and she told me, "I always have to find a way that makes sense to me and this is what makes sense to me for this problem." I want all children to have this feeling. Creating is what lies beyond understanding. That is what we see happening when children generate conjectures or use relational thinking to reason about a number sentence or come up with a strategy to solve a problem. Children's creations, their conjectures and ways of thinking, become part of them. I want all children to have these creations and feel that they are problem solvers.

Mazie Jenkins, Mathematics resource teacher

1 | DEVELOPING MATHEMATICAL THINKING

Learning mathematics involves learning ways of thinking. It involves learning powerful mathematical ideas rather than a collection of disconnected procedures for carrying out calculations. But it also entails learning how to generate those ideas, how to express them using words and symbols, and how to justify to oneself and to others that those ideas are true. Elementary school children are capable of learning how to engage in this type of mathematical thinking, but often they are not given the opportunity to do so. In the chapters that follow, we portray how elementary school students can be encouraged to make explicit the powerful, unifying ideas of mathematics. We illustrate how they construct representations of those ideas in order to examine them and to communicate them, and we consider how students struggle to justify that the ideas are true.

INTEGRATING ARITHMETIC AND ALGEBRA

Arithmetic is and will continue to be a major focus of the elementary school curriculum. But we need to reconsider how arithmetic is taught and learned. Often the learning of arithmetic is isolated from other related mathematical ideas. The artificial separation of arithmetic and algebra deprives students of powerful ways of thinking about mathematics in the early grades and makes it more difficult for them to learn algebra in the later grades. Understanding takes a long time to develop. The kind of mathematical thinking that can provide a foundation for learning algebra must be developed over an extended period of time, starting in the early elementary grades. In the chapters that follow, we discuss how to help children build on their implicit knowledge of arithmetic to provide a foundation for learning algebra. This does not mean simply using the current high school algebra curriculum in elementary school. To the contrary, rather than teaching algebra procedures to elementary school children, our goal is to support them in developing ways of thinking about arithmetic that are more consistent with the ways that students have to think to learn algebra successfully.

These ways of thinking both pave the way for learning algebra and enhance the learning of arithmetic.

If students genuinely understand arithmetic at a level at which they can explain and justify the properties they are using as they carry out calculations, they have learned some critical foundations of algebra. Unfortunately, the way that most students learn arithmetic does not provide a foundation for learning algebra. For many students, arithmetic is perceived as a series of calculations. Students do not think much about the properties of number that make the calculations possible. Consequently, when they begin to study algebra, they do not see that the procedures they are using to solve equations and simplify expressions are based on the same properties of number that they have used in arithmetic. Even worse, the conceptions of arithmetic that many students bring to algebra can actually get in the way of their learning algebra. It does not have to be that way. Children can learn arithmetic in a way that provides a basis for learning algebra.

> Many adults equate school algebra with symbol manipulation—solving complicated equations and simplifying algebraic expressions. Indeed, the algebraic symbols and the procedures for working with them are a towering, historic mathematical accomplishment and are critical in mathematical work. But algebra is more than moving symbols around. Students need to understand the concepts of algebra, the structures and principles that govern the manipulation of the symbols, and how the symbols themselves can be used for recording ideas and gaining insights into situations. (National Council of Teachers of Mathematics, 2000, p. 37)

The fundamental properties that children use in carrying out arithmetic calculations provide the basis for most of the symbolic manipulation in algebra. For example, when children use their knowledge of simple arithmetic combinations to add multiples of ten, they are implicitly using a basic property that relates addition and multiplication. For example, a student might explain: "Fifty plus 30 equals 80, because 5 plus 3 equals 8, so 5 tens plus 3 tens is 8 tens, or 80." Symbolically, this can be represented as:

$$50 + 30 = 5 \times 10 + 3 \times 10 = (5 + 3) \times 10 = 8 \times 10 = 80$$

The same basic reasoning applies to simplifying algebraic expressions: $5b + 3b = 8b$, because $5b + 3b$ means 5 times b added to 3 times b. Represented symbolically:

$$5b + 3b = (5 + 3)b = 8b$$
or equivalently $5 \times b + 3 \times b = (5 + 3) \times b = 8 \times b$

Thus, understanding addition of multidigit numbers can provide a foundation for students to understand the principles that they will use to simplify algebraic expressions.

Focusing on fundamental properties of number and number operations also makes the learning of arithmetic more efficient and provides students with more powerful and flexible ways to apply the arithmetic they learn. Students who are successful in mathematics are not simply better at computing or manipulating symbols. By making generalizations and recognizing relationships among concepts and procedures, these students have less to learn and frequently are able to simplify their calculations. For example, students who understand the relation between multiplication and division can draw on this knowledge to simplify the learning of multiplication and division number facts. They can use what they know about 9×7 to figure out $63 \div 9$. Similarly, students who recognize that they can reorder and regroup numbers when they add them can simplify the calculation $75 + 48 + 25$ by first adding the 75 and the 25.

STRUCTURE OF THE BOOK

We start by considering what children already know about fundamental properties of arithmetic and how they may use this knowledge to solve problems. Initially students are given the opportunity to use basic properties of arithmetic without explicitly identifying the properties they are using. Next we consider how to engage students in articulating conjectures about properties that they think are true and provide them opportunity and the means to express these conjectures clearly and accurately using words and symbols. In the concluding chapters, we examine how students learn to justify that the conjectures they have proposed are true and how to use them to show that the computational (and ultimately algebraic) procedures they use are valid.

What Children Know

We begin by examining some of the conceptions and misconceptions that students bring to learning mathematics throughout the elementary grades. Most students have some informal knowledge about basic properties of arithmetic, and we can build on this knowledge as we try to help students articulate fundamental ideas of arithmetic. Students also bring some conceptions about mathematics and the use of symbols that are not entirely accurate and need to be addressed so that they do not get in the way of students' learning. In Chapter 2, we consider how to address a common misconception about the meaning of the equal sign (see Box 1.1). In Chapter 3, we look at how students can use basic properties of arithmetic to simplify calculations. We initially focus on helping children look for relations among numbers and number operations using basic properties of arithmetic (see Box 1.1). The emphasis is on providing opportunities for children to begin to think about the properties of operations and relations rather than calculating by rote. At this point, the discussion is relatively informal, and children are not asked to be explicit about the number properties they are using to simplify calculations and express relations.

BOX 1.1 *Thinking About Relations and Equality*

Consider how one second-grade student, Robin, solved the following problem:

$$18 + 27 = \square + 29$$

Robin: Twenty-nine is two more than 27, so the number in the box has to be two less than 18 to make the two sides equal. So it's 16.

Robin's response is notable in several ways. First, Robin recognized that the equal sign represented a relation between the two expressions on either side of the equal sign. Many children throughout the elementary and middle grades, and even into high school, think that the equal sign should be followed by the answer to the calculation on the left side of the equal sign. For the above problem, they would respond that 45 should go in the box. Although this error is common, it represents a serious misconception that is incompatible with the way that the equal sign is used in algebra, and it limits students' learning of arithmetic. One of the keys to developing mathematical thinking is to understand that the equal sign expresses a relation.

Another notable feature of Robin's response is that she did not actually carry out the indicated calculations. She could have responded correctly by first computing the sum of 18 and 27 and then figuring out what number to add to 29 to get 45. But she recognized that it was not necessary to do the calculation. Instead she compared the numbers in the expressions and realized that because 29 was two more than 27, the number added to it had to be two less than 18 to make both expressions equal. Rather than carrying out the indicated calculations, she looked for relations between the expressions that could simplify the calculation. For Robin, the expression 18 + 27 did not just represent an arithmetic procedure to be carried out; the expression itself was an object of reflection that could be compared directly to the expression $\square$ + 29. This type of thinking is critical in algebra, and it can enrich the learning of arithmetic and allow students to be more flexible in applying their computational skills.

Making Generalizations Explicit and Expressing Them Using Words and Symbols

The procedures we use to add, subtract, multiply, divide, and compare numbers are based on a small number of fundamental properties of number and number operations, and much of algebra is based on the same basic properties. When students clearly understand these properties and how they apply to the mathematics they learn, they have acquired the basis for understanding arithmetic and algebra. As children learn arithmetic, they implicitly use a number of these fundamental properties. For example, when young children add a larger number to a smaller number, they often count on from the larger number even though the smaller number comes first. To add 3 + 8, they count on "8, [*pause*] 9, 10, 11." By counting on from the larger number, children essentially change the order of the numbers they add. This example suggests that, as early as first grade, many children have some implicit knowledge of an important property of addition, and they use this property and a number of other properties in carrying out their calculations.

Our goal is to make these properties the explicit focus of attention so that

- all students have access to basic mathematical properties;
- students understand why the computation procedures they use work the way they do;
- students apply their procedures flexibly in a variety of contexts; and
- students recognize the connections between arithmetic and algebra and can use their understanding of arithmetic as a foundation for learning algebra with understanding.

We not only want to make explicit the fundamental properties of arithmetic; we want students to learn the importance of expressing them precisely and accurately using words and symbols. In Chapter 4, we discuss how students can be encouraged to articulate explicitly conjectures about basic number properties and how they may engage in discussion to refine the wording of their conjectures. Symbols provide a concise and precise means of representing basic properties about number operations and relations. In Chapters 5 and 6, we discuss how students can be introduced to symbolic notation that they can use for this purpose. The symbols of algebra play a dual role in students' learning. Students use symbols to represent basic properties of arithmetic, and students use these properties to simplify symbolic expressions and solve equations.

> **COMMUNICATION STANDARD**
>
> Instructional programs from prekindergarten through grade 12 should enable all students to—
>
> - organize and consolidate their mathematical thinking through communication;
> - communicate their mathematical thinking coherently and clearly to peers, teachers, and others;
> - analyze and evaluate the mathematical thinking of others;
> - use the language of mathematics to express mathematical ideas precisely.
>
> (NCTM, 2000, p. 60)

Justifying Mathematical Statements and Procedures

One of the key components of understanding is being able to explain why a procedure works or why a particular statement is true. There are standards in mathematics for deciding whether a mathematical statement is true or not. An important goal of mathematics instruction is to help students address how disputes in mathematics are resolved and understand what is required to show that a mathematical statement is true. This is the goal of Chapters 7, 8, and 9.

ENGAGING IN THE PRACTICES OF MATHEMATICS

We have found that students who learn to articulate and justify their own mathematical ideas, reason through their own and others' mathematical explanations, and provide a rationale for their answers develop a deep understanding that is critical to their future success in mathematics and related fields. Students not only need to learn the big ideas of mathematics; they need to learn the mathematical ways of thinking that are entailed in generating these ideas, in deciding how to express them, in justifying that they are true, and in using them to justify the mathematical procedures they are learning. They can learn these ways of thinking only by engaging in them.

Algebra is sometimes characterized as generalized arithmetic. We are proposing that the teaching and learning of arithmetic be conceived as the foundation for algebra. Our goal is to develop ways of thinking about mathematics and of engaging in discussion about mathematics that are more productive both for learning arithmetic and for smoothing the transition to learning algebra. Algebra often serves as a gatekeeper that prevents students from continuing the study of mathematics, thereby limiting their access to college majors and careers that require knowledge of mathematics beyond simple arithmetic. Developing mathematical thinking in the elementary grades puts students on a path to learning mathematics with understanding so that algebra is a gateway to opportunity, not a gate that blocks their way.

REASONING AND PROOF STANDARD

Instructional programs from prekindergarten through grade 12 should enable all students to—

- recognize reasoning and proof as fundamental aspects of mathematics;
- make and investigate mathematical conjectures;
- develop and evaluate mathematical arguments and proofs;
- select and use various types of reasoning and methods of proof.

(NCTM, 2000, p. 56)

REFERENCE

NATIONAL COUNCIL OF TEACHERS OF MATHEMATICS (NCTM). 2000. *Principles and Standards for School Mathematics*. Reston, VA: National Council of Teachers of Mathematics.

TEACHER COMMENTARY 1.1

Mathematics is in everyone's life and should be a part of everyone's life. Unfortunately, there is a gate to higher-level mathematics and it keeps certain kids out. Not enough kids are taking higher-level math courses and it tends to be our disadvantaged kids who are losing out. This gate must be opened so that higher-level mathematics is available and reachable for everyone. One way to open this gate is by talking about big ideas in the early grades instead of waiting until the upper grades. By middle and high school we have turned many kids off mathematics. Kids have already decided that either they don't like math anymore, or they don't understand math, or they can't do math. The kids who have always been the mathematicians of the world have known implicitly the big ideas; it is just a part of them. There has also been a group of kids who had inklings of the big ideas but didn't develop their understanding of them. And then we have a group of kids who maybe didn't think about big ideas. These kids might not have even realized that there were big ideas in mathematics. One thing that is so helpful to all the children I teach is that we have a lot of conversations so that the big ideas are made explicit. The kids who have these ideas are putting them out there and, as they do so, clarifying their ideas. When the ideas get expressed, the kids who had the inklings are making relational bridges to the ideas they have and these ideas continue to develop. The kids who have never thought about these big ideas start to think about them; a seed has been planted. The more you talk about these ideas, the more the mathematics makes sense to them. I think there is growth in all kids when you talk about the big ideas.

Annie Keith, Second- and third-grade teacher

2 | EQUALITY

How would the students in your class respond to the following question:

What number would you put in the box to make this a true number sentence?

$8 + 4 = \square + 5$

If they are like most elementary students, they will not immediately respond that the answer is 7. Two common responses likely will be 12 and 17. Results from students in thirty typical elementary-grade classes are summarized in Table 2.1.

Response/Percent Responding[1]				
Grade	7	12	17	12 and 17
1 and 2	5	58	13	8
3 and 4	9	49	25	10
5 and 6	2	76	21	2

TABLE 2.1
*Percent of Students
Offering Various
Solutions to*
$8 + 4 = \square + 5$

[1]From Falkner, Levi, & Carpenter, 1999.

Fewer than 10 percent of the students in any grade gave the correct response of 7, and strikingly, performance did not improve with age. In fact, in this sample, results for the sixth-grade students were actually slightly worse than the results for students in the earlier grades. These data illustrate that many, if not most, elementary school students harbor serious misconceptions about the meaning of the equal sign. Most elementary students, and many older students as well, do not understand that the equal sign denotes the relation between two equal quantities. Rather, they interpret the equal sign as a command to carry out a calculation, much as a calculator does when we press the equal sign. This misconception limits students' ability to learn basic arithmetic ideas with understanding and their flexibility in representing and using those ideas, and it creates even more serious problems as they move to algebra.

In the remainder of this chapter, we discuss students' conceptions of the meaning of the equal sign and consider briefly the potential sources of children's misconceptions. A primary objective of the chapter is to think about how we might engage children in examining and revising their conceptions of the meaning of the equal sign. We also examine in more depth what children's errors tell us about their understanding of basic mathematical principles. The good news is that we can make a significant difference in helping children interpret the equal sign in appropriate ways. Furthermore, discussions with students about their conceptions of what the equal sign means offer an ideal opportunity to begin to engage them in discussions that illustrate how mathematical ideas emerge and how mathematical disputes are resolved.

CHILDREN'S CONCEPTIONS OF THE MEANING OF THE EQUAL SIGN

Following are five typical responses to the problem given at the beginning of the chapter. The responses illustrate quite different conceptions of what the equal sign means.

Lucy: The Answer Comes Next

Ms. L.: Can you tell me what number you would put in the box to make this a true number sentence?

$8 + 4 = \square + 5$

Lucy: [*After a brief period*] Twelve.

Ms. L.: How do you know it is 12?

Lucy: Because that's the answer; 8 and 4 are 12. See, I counted, 8 [*pause*] 9, 10, 11, 12. See, that's 12.

Ms. L.: What about this 5 over here? [*Pointing to the 5 in the number sentence*]

Lucy: That's just there.

Ms. L.: Do you have to do anything with it?

Lucy: No. It's just there. It doesn't have anything to do with the 8 and 4.

Ms. L.: What do you think it means?

Lucy: I don't know. I don't think it means anything. Maybe they just put it there to confuse us. You know, sometimes Ms. J. puts extra numbers in story problems to make us think about what to add or subtract.

For Lucy, the equal sign meant the answer came next, and the answer was the answer to the operation that came right before the equal sign. The equal sign was a command to carry out the calculation; it did not represent a relation between the numbers represented by 8 + 4 and □ + 5.

Randy: Use All the Numbers

Randy: It's 17.
Ms. L.: How did you figure 17?
Randy: Because I know that 8 and 4 is 12, and 5 more is 17.
Ms. L.: Why did you add all those numbers?
Randy: Because it says to add. See. [*Points to the two + symbols*]
Ms. L.: Okay. But these two numbers are over here on this side of the equal sign [*points at the 8 + 4*] and the 5 is over here [*points at the 5*].
Randy: Yeah, but you have to add all the numbers. That's what it says to do.

Randy took into account all the numbers, but he did not recognize that where the symbols appeared in the number sentence made a difference. The only way he could think of to use all the numbers was to add them all together.

Barb: Extend the Problem

Barb: [*Puts 12 in the box and then writes = 17 after the 5 (8 + 4 = 12 + 5 = 17).*]
Ms. L.: Can you tell me what you did?
Barb: Sure. I did 8 plus 4, and that's 12, and then I had to add the 5, so that made 17.
Ms. L.: Does 8 plus 4 equal 12 plus 5?
Barb: 8 and 4 is 12 and you add the 5 to get 17.

What Barb did made perfect sense to her. Like Lucy, she carried out the calculation before the equal sign and wrote the answer in the box. Like Lucy, she also believed that the number after the equal sign represented the calculation to the left. But like Randy, she then wanted to take into account the 5, so she added it to the 12 and put the answer at the end of the number sentence after a second equal sign. She was using the equal signs to show sequences of calculations. She certainly did not consider whether 8 + 4 was equal to 17. Even adults sometimes use this type of notation when more than two numbers are combined in different ways. This, however, is an incorrect use of the equal sign.

Making Sense

Lucy, Randy, and Barb all had different ways of making sense of the number sentence they were asked to solve. Their methods were not unreasonable attempts to deal with an unfamiliar problem. In virtually all of the number sentences that Lucy and Barb had encountered up to that time, the answer always came right after the equal sign. They generalized from their experience that one of the "rules" for writing number sentences was that the answer comes right after the equal sign. Randy made a different generalization. He overgeneralized a valid property of addition to presume that the order of the symbols in a number sentence is not important. In fact, Randy appeared to think that, for all practical purposes, the equal sign was irrelevant.

In all three cases, the errors were errors of syntax, errors in the children's interpretation of the rules of how the equal sign is used to express relations between two numbers. The children could figure out that $8 + 4$ and $7 + 5$ both are equal to 12. But they interpreted $8 + 4$ as an operation to be carried out rather than as one way to represent 12, and for them the equal sign signified that the answer was to be calculated and written to the right of the equal sign.

TEACHER COMMENTARY 2.1

My students struggle a lot with the equal sign, but it is a good struggle. I want my first graders to understand that "equal" doesn't mean "the answer comes next." At the beginning of the year I gave my students $8 + 4 = \square + 7$ and they all said 12. They completely ignored the $+ 7$. So I asked them, "What about this plus 7?"

About half of them said, "Oh, plus 7 equals 19."

Now it is December and some kids are starting to let go of the idea that "equals" means "the answer comes next." They all understand equality in concrete terms. If I have 4 red blocks and 5 green blocks on one plate and only 6 yellow blocks on the other plate, they all can figure out how to add blocks to the second plate to make the number of blocks on the two plates equal. Some kids might use a lot of trial and error to figure that out, but they can do it. It's not that they don't understand making things equal; it's using the equal sign that is the difficulty. We will continue to struggle; it is important that they understand the equal sign. Right from the beginning of first grade I will write things like $12 = 6 + 6$ or $3 = 3$ so that they can see the different ways to use the equal sign.

Dawn Michaels, First-grade teacher

The fact that these children's misconceptions revolve around the appropriate use of symbols rather than failure to understand relations among quantities does not, however, mean that the misconceptions are trivial or are easily overcome. In fact, children may cling tenaciously to the conceptions they have formed about how the equal sign should be used, and simply explaining the correct use of the symbol is not sufficient to convince most children to abandon their prior conceptions and adopt the accepted use of the equal sign. Before we consider how to challenge children's misconceptions about the meaning of the equal sign, however, we should look at the responses to the same problem of two children who recognize that the equal sign represents a relation between two numbers.

Ricardo: [*After a short pause*] It's 7.

Ms. L.:   How do you know that it's 7?

Ricardo: Well, 8 and 4 is 12. So I had to figure out what to go with 5 to make 12, and I figured out that had to be 7.

Ms. L.:   So why did you want to figure out what to put with 5 to make 12?

Ricardo: Because I had 12 over here [*pointing to the left of the equal sign*], so I had to have 12 over here [*pointing to the right side of the equal sign*]. And 5 and 7 is 12.

Ms. L.:   Some kids have told me that 12 should go in the box. What do you think about that?

Ricardo: That's not right. Twelve and 5—that would be 17, and that's not equal to 12. These two sides have got to be the same.

Gina: [*Very quickly*] Seven.

Ms. L.:   How do you know that it's 7?

Gina: Well, I saw that the 5 over here [*pointing to the 5 in the number sentence*] was one more than the 4 over here [*pointing to the 4 in the number sentence*], so the number in the box had to be one less than the 8. So it's 7.

Ms. L.:   That's very interesting. Let's try another one. How about:

$$57 + 86 = \Box + 84$$

Gina: [*Almost immediately*] That's easy. Fifty-nine.

Ms. L.:   Wow. That was quick.

Gina: Yeah. It's just like the other one. It's just two more, because the 84 is two less.

Both Ricardo and Gina viewed the equal sign as expressing a relation between numbers. The expressions on both sides of the equal sign had to represent the same number. Critically, they did not impose other arbitrary rules that number sentences had to follow a certain form. They were comfortable with expressions involving addition (or other combinations of operations) on either side of the equal sign. In contrast, many students believe that number sentences should follow a certain form with an operation on the left and the answer on the right. When they encounter different forms of number sentences, such as $8 + 4 = \Box + 5$, students like Lucy, Randy, and Barb are forced to adapt their rules to respond to an unfamiliar context, and their adaptations often involve calculating answers rather than looking for relations.

Ricardo calculated the sum on the left side of the equation and found a number to put in the box that when added to 5 would give the same number. Gina recognized both that she was looking for a relation between

2.1

the two sides of the equation and that a relation among the numbers in the two expressions made it unnecessary for her to actually carry out the calculations. Although both Gina and Ricardo demonstrated that they understood the appropriate use of the equal sign, Gina's strategy shows greater understanding and more flexibility than Ricardo's does. Gina considered the relation between the two addition expressions in the equation, not just the relation between the answers to the two calculations. She was able to consider 8 + 4 as more than a calculation to be carried out. This ability to reflect on relations among mathematical expressions such as 8 + 4 and □ + 5 is critical for students to think more generally about arithmetic and to extend their knowledge of arithmetic to algebra.

Without further probing, we cannot be sure that Ricardo could not solve the problem as Gina did. With small numbers children often will either know the answer or carry out the calculation even though they could compare the expressions without calculating. It generally is easier to observe whether children actually need to calculate when larger numbers are used.

DEVELOPING CHILDREN'S CONCEPTIONS OF EQUALITY

In order to help children develop an appropriate conception of equality, we have found that it is productive to put them in a position to challenge their existing conceptions. This can be accomplished by engaging them in discussions in which different conceptions of the equal sign emerge and must be resolved. In these discussions, which may occur either in a whole-class setting or in smaller groups, students can be encouraged to clearly articulate their conceptions of how the equal sign is used and to make them explicit so that the other members of the class can understand the different perspectives represented in the class. It is necessary for students to be clear about their conceptions of the equal sign and what supports those conceptions in order to attempt to figure out how to resolve the differences.

These discussions both address students' conceptions of the meaning of the equal sign and represent a first step in developing ways of thinking and conversing that embody the principles of algebraic reasoning. The contradictions between students' different conceptions of the meaning of the equal sign provide a context in which they need to examine and resolve inconsistencies. In discussing alternative conceptions of the equal sign, students are put in a position in which they need to articulate mathematical principles that often are left implicit. They must justify the principles that they propose in ways that convince others, and they must recognize and resolve conflicting assumptions and conclusions.

A Context for Discussing the Equal Sign

We have found that it is most fruitful to engage students in a discussion of the equal sign in the context of specific tasks. Appropriately chosen tasks can (a) provide a focus for students to articulate their ideas, (b) challenge students' conceptions by providing different contexts in which they need to examine the positions they have staked out, and (c) provide a window on children's thinking. True/false and open number sentences have proven particularly productive as a context for discussing equality. These number sentences can be manipulated in a variety of ways to create situations that may challenge students' conceptions and provide a context for discussion. At the beginning of this chapter, we saw how the open number sentence $8 + 4 = \square + 5$ generated a variety of responses that, in a classroom discussion, could provide a basis for considering alternative perspectives of the meaning of the equal sign. It is not easy, however, to resolve these different perspectives. The use of the equal sign is a matter of convention, and students cannot actually discover the convention or decide which perspective is right entirely by logic. However, a variety of contexts may encourage students to examine the positions they have taken.

True/False Number Sentences

Students may not have experience with true/false number sentences, but it is relatively easy to introduce them. We have found that it is not necessary to engage students in a general discussion about true/false number sentences or what it means for a number sentence to be true or false. It seems to work best to provide an example and ask whether the number sentence is true or false. It is a good idea to start with number sentences that involve relatively simple calculations with a single number to the right of the equal sign. Children quickly pick up the critical ideas in the context of talking about specific true/false number sentences, as in the following example.

Mr. B.: Is this number sentence true or false: $8 - 5 = 3$?

Students: True.

Mr. B.: How do you all know that it is true? Maria.

Maria: Because 8 minus 5 is 3.

Mr. B.: Okay. How about this one, is this number sentence true or false: $3 \times 4 = 15$?

Chiang: No. That's false, because 3×4 is 12, and that's not equal to 15.

Mr. B.: Anybody disagree with Chiang? Okay, let's try another one, how about $587 + 468 = 1,055$?

For this problem, the children had to calculate the sum, but after a short time they concluded that this was a true number sentence because the sum they calculated was equal to 1,055.

Although these number sentences do not require students to supply the answer after the equal sign, they fit the form that students are familiar with in that there is a single number after the equal sign, and students generally do not have much difficulty deciding whether they are true or false. Once students are familiar with true/false number sentences, number sentences can be introduced that may encourage them to examine their conceptions of the meaning of the equal sign. Juxtaposing number sentences that students agree are true with those that are not in the familiar form may challenge some students' conceptions of how the equal sign is used. Following are several collections of problems that may bring out different perspectives on equality. Although the examples are shown with addition, number sentences with the same structure could be written for the other three operations as well.

a. $3 + 5 = 8$
b. $8 = 3 + 5$
c. $8 = 8$
d. $3 + 5 = 3 + 5$
e. $3 + 5 = 5 + 3$
f. $3 + 5 = 4 + 4$

Except for the first number sentence in the sequence, none of these examples follows the familiar form with an operation on two numbers on the left of the equal sign, which is followed directly by the answer. Asking students to choose whether each number sentence is true or false can encourage them to examine their assumptions about the equal sign. They generally agree that the numbers represented by the expressions on either side of the equal sign are the same, but they may still believe that these are not true number sentences; they often persist in asserting that you just cannot write it that way. These situations, however, often start to cause them some conflict if they do not view the equal sign as expressing a relation meaning *the same number as*.

Most students will agree that the first sentence is true and that sentence provides a base of comparison for the other number sentences. They may not be so sure about the second, and they can be engaged in a discussion of how the two number sentences differ and why they do not believe the second is true. Comparing these sentences may help students to articulate the specific rules they are using to decide whether a sentence is true or false. They may, for example, say that there should just be a single number after the equal sign. In that case, Sentence c may encourage them to further examine their assumptions. If they respond that there have to be two numbers on the left of the equal sign, the number sentence $3 + 5 = 3 + 5$ might provide a context for students to examine that assertion. Students often will agree that $3 + 5 = 3 + 5$ is true because "there are the same numbers on both sides of the equal sign." Sentence e provides a slightly different context for thinking about this claim.

Including zero in a number sentence may encourage students to accept a number sentence in which more than one number appears after the equal sign. For example, consider the following sequence of number sentences:

a. $9 + 5 = 14$
b. $9 + 5 = 14 + 0$
c. $9 + 5 = 0 + 14$
d. $9 + 5 = 13 + 1$

Once again most students will agree that the first sentence is true. Initially it may be easier for some students to accept Sentence b than Sentence d. For one thing, the "answer" to 9 + 5 appears right after the equal sign, and most students are familiar with the effect of adding zero. As a consequence, a number of students who would not accept Sentence d as true may accept Sentence b as true. This opens the door to having more than a single number after the equal sign. Sentence c offers an additional challenge. The "answer" no longer appears right after the equal sign, but the only difference between Sentences b and c is that the order of the numbers has been changed, and most students recognize that changing the order of numbers that they are adding does not change the answer. Thus, a comparison of Sentences b and c may provide an additional challenge to the rules that students impose on the use of the equal sign. If students are willing to accept Sentences a, b, and c as true, many of the reasons that they would give for not accepting Sentence d have already been eliminated. This can result in a potentially productive discussion about the necessity of applying rules consistently.

Open number sentences can be written to illustrate many of the same ideas. The question is: "What number can you put in the box to make this number sentence true?" Many numbers can be substituted for the box in each of the following number sentences, but only one makes the number sentence true. This way of talking about open number sentences provides a link among true/false and open number sentences. Following are open number sentences corresponding to the first collection of true/false number sentences:

> *a.* $3 + 5 = \square$ *or* $3 + \square = 8$
> *b.* $8 = 3 + \square$ *or* $\square = 3 + 5$
> *c.* $8 = \square$
> *d.* $3 + 5 = \square + 5$
> *e.* $3 + 5 = \square + 3$
> *f.* $3 + 5 = \square + 4$

These open number sentences, or similar problems with different numbers, might be given after the corresponding true/false question to follow up on the ideas that came out of the discussion of the true/false number sentence. We have found that students sometimes respond differently to true/false and open number sentences. Some students who have appeared to understand that the equal sign represents a relation when deciding whether a number sentence is true or false revert to calculating the answer to the left of the equal sign when they see number sentences like d, e, and f in the previous list.

Wording and Notation

We are trying to help students understand that the equal sign signifies a relation between two numbers. It sometimes is useful to use words that express that relation more directly: "Eight is the same amount as 3 plus 5." Some

TEACHER COMMENTARY 2.2

Changing students' conceptions about the equal sign is not easy, as illustrated by this commentary written by a primary-grade teacher.

My purpose for this lesson was to increase the children's comfort level with number sentences that had a single number on the left side of the equal sign and an expression involving two numbers and a plus or minus sign on the right side. Midway through the lesson I wrote the following number sentence and asked if it was true or false: 4 + 3 = 7. The children answered that it was true. Then I wrote this problem: 7 = 4 + 3. This time the children weren't nearly so sure, but eventually they decided that the sentence was true. At this point a child suggested that I write 3 + 4 = 7. There was much discussion over whether that number sentence was the same or different from the first one I'd written. Generally the children did not have the language to discuss whether 4 + 3 was the same as 3 + 4, and why they thought it was or wasn't. I think the children simply considered that since the number order was different, it was a different number sentence. In any event, all children agreed that his number sentence was true.

At this point the three number sentences were on the board, each one under the other like this:

4 + 3 = 7

7 = 4 + 3

3 + 4 = 7

Since we had been talking about the equal sign, I considered this a golden opportunity to pose the following open number sentence: 3 + 4 = ☐ + 3. My question was, "What goes in the box?" Those children who were already comfortable with the meaning of the equal sign said 4, but the loudest response was 7!

Karen Falkner, First- and second-grade teacher

teachers also have found it useful to use notation that shows that the numbers on the two sides of the equal sign represent the same numerical value:

$$8 + 4 \quad = \quad 7 + 5 \quad or \quad 8 + 4 = 7 + 5$$
$$\diagdown\diagup \qquad \diagdown\diagup \qquad\qquad \| \quad \|$$
$$12 \qquad\quad 12 \qquad\qquad 12 = 12$$

Classroom Interactions

2.3

Although the selection of tasks can provide a context for engaging students in examining their conceptions of the meaning of the equal sign, the nature of the discussion of mathematical ideas is critical. The goal is not just to teach students appropriate conceptions of the use of the equal sign; it is equally important to engage them in productive mathematical arguments.

Discussing alternative conceptions of the meaning of the equal sign can challenge students to examine the warrants that justify their claims. "Why do you think that?" "Why do you think that you cannot write number sentences that look like that?" Helping students understand the accepted use of the equal sign represents the first step in helping students make and justify generalizations about mathematics. The discussion of different conceptions of the equal sign and the ways that those differences are resolved can set the stage for beginning to help students understand the importance of carefully articulating and justifying mathematical claims. These discussions can provide opportunities for students to reflect upon and make sense of their ideas and to differentiate them from contrasting ideas of other students. They also can consider and evaluate the consequences of these ideas. We want children to see that there are different meanings held by different members of the class and that not all the meanings can be correct. The issue is not just to figure out what is correct but also to come to understand how fundamental differences get negotiated and resolved.

BENCHMARKS

Children do not necessarily pass through a sequence of distinct stages in developing their conceptions of the equal sign, and it should not be presumed that all children follow the same path to understanding how the equal sign is used. There are, however, some benchmarks to work toward as children's conception of the equal sign evolves.

1. Getting children to be specific about what they think the equal sign means represents a first step in changing their conceptions. In order for children to compare and contrast different conceptions, they need to be clear about what their conceptions are. This means getting beyond just comparing the different answers to a problem like $8 + 4 = \square + 5$. Some children may say that the equal sign must be preceded by two numbers joined by a plus or a minus and followed by the answer (resulting in an answer of 12 to this problem). Others may say that you have to use all the numbers (resulting in an answer of 17 to this problem). Even though neither of these conceptions is correct, getting them clearly articulated represents progress and provides a basis for challenging them.

2. The second benchmark is achieved when children first accept as true some number sentence that is not of the form $a + b = c$. It may be something like $8 = 5 + 3$, $8 = 8$, $3 + 5 = 8 + 0$, or $3 + 5 = 3 + 5$.

3. The third benchmark is achieved when children recognize that the equal sign represents a relation between two equal numbers. At this point they compare the two sides of the equal sign by carrying out the calculations on each side of the equal sign. Ricardo's response is representative of this benchmark.

4. The fourth benchmark is achieved when children are able to compare the mathematical expressions without actually carrying out the

calculations. Gina's response is representative of this benchmark. The development of this type of reasoning is discussed in the next chapter.

These benchmarks are a guide. Not all children in any given class will attain these benchmarks at the same time, and not all children will follow this exact sequence. In fact, we have found that some children use relational thinking characteristic of level 4 as they are beginning to learn that the equal sign represents a relation between two numbers. Throughout the elementary grades, most classes initially will have a great deal of variability in the conceptions that students hold as they are striving to attain an understanding of the use of the equal sign.

WHAT TO AVOID

Frequently the equal sign is used as a shorthand for a variety of purposes. It is a good idea to avoid using the equal sign in ways that do not represent a relation between numbers. Table 2.2 includes several examples of uses of the equal sign that should be avoided.

TABLE 2.2
Inappropriate Uses of the Equal Sign

1. Listing the ages or some other numerical characteristic of people or things:
   John = 8, Marcie = 9, etc.

2. Designating the number of objects in a collection:

3. Using equality to represent a string of calculations:
   $20 + 30 = 50 + 7 = 57 + 8 = 65$

4. Using equality between two pictures:

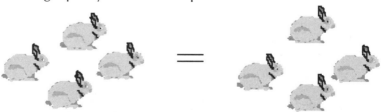

In the first example, John is not a number. His age may be 8 or he may have scored 8 points in a game, but we should avoid using the equal sign to show this correspondence. The equal sign should be reserved to show the relation between numbers or expressions representing numbers. A similar concern applies to Examples 2 and 4. The number of objects in the collection is 6, but the set itself is not equal to the number 6. A group of six children is not equal to another group of six children. There is the same number of people in the two groups, but the groups themselves are not the same, and we should avoid using the equal sign in this way. It is tempting to use the equal sign to represent a series of calculations, as in the third example, but it is easy to see how that can reinforce some of the misconceptions illustrated at the beginning of this chapter. Rather than using the equal sign in this case, it is preferable to use write a longer version that emphasizes the correct use of the equal sign:

$$20 + 30 = 50$$

$$50 + 7 = 57$$

$$57 + 8 = 65$$

Once children begin to understand that the equal sign signifies a relation between numbers, it is important to continue to provide number sentences in a variety of forms and not to fall back to using only number sentences with the answer coming after the equal sign. Children's conceptions of how to use the equal sign tend to be fragile, and they continue to need experiences with number sentences that challenge them to think about the equal sign as signifying a relation rather than a signal to calculate an answer.

THE USE OF THE EQUAL SIGN IS A CONVENTION

In helping children to develop an understanding of the equal sign as expressing a relation, it is necessary to keep in mind that the way that the equal sign is used in mathematics is a matter of agreement and convention. Many properties of mathematics are not simply conventions. For example, the fact that the order of the numbers in an addition problem can be interchanged (the commutative property, e.g. $6 + 5 = 5 + 6$) is not simply a matter of convention, and in later chapters we will discuss how students can show that this property holds for all numbers. But it is not possible to justify that the equal sign represents a relation rather than a command to do something. If a student insists that you just cannot write number sentences that way, that it is not allowed, there is no way to refute that assertion directly. We can, however, ask the student to justify his or her claim that number sentences cannot be written that way. This can open the doors to a discussion of what should be taken as evidence for a claim. Is it sufficient to presume that something is true because all the examples one has seen support that claim? Essentially, students are making claims about conventions, and the question is, how do they know that they have adopted the convention that is accepted by everyone else?

An important feature of conventions in mathematics is consistency. Once a convention has been agreed upon, it has to be applied consistently. Asking students to consider the implications of their conceptions of the equal sign for a variety of different forms of number sentences begins to put them in touch with this feature of mathematical thinking.

SMOOTHING THE TRANSITION TO ALGEBRA

A limited conception of what the equal sign means is one of the major stumbling blocks in learning algebra. Virtually all manipulations on equations require understanding that the equal sign represents a relation. Consider, for example, the procedures for solving an equation like $5x + 32 = 97$. First one might subtract 32 from each side of the equation (or add -32). That requires understanding that the equal sign expresses a relation and that adding or subtracting the same thing to two expressions preserves the equality. When 32 is subtracted from both sides of the equation, the equation becomes $5x + 32 - 32 = 97 - 32$. What kind of meaning can students who exhibit the kinds of misconceptions of the equal sign illustrated at the beginning of this chapter attribute to this equation? With a limited conception of the equal sign as an instruction to carry out the preceding calculation, one is limited to carrying out arithmetic calculations. Understanding that the equal sign represents a relation between equal numbers opens up the power of algebra for representing problems and performing complex operations on mathematical expressions. This can enrich the learning of arithmetic as well as the learning of algebra.

WHERE DO CHILDREN'S MISCONCEPTIONS ABOUT THE EQUAL SIGN COME FROM?

It is difficult to sort out exactly why misconceptions about the meaning of the equal sign are so pervasive and so persistent. A good guess is that many children see only examples of number sentences with an operation to the left of the equal sign and the answer on the right, and they overgeneralize from those limited examples. But that is not the whole story. We have worked with kindergarten and first-grade children who have had limited exposure to number sentences of any kind but still strongly believed that the equal sign had to be followed immediately by the result of the calculation. Nevertheless, limiting children's exposure to a narrow range of number sentences does appear to contribute to students' misconceptions about the equal sign. In fact, we have found that even after students develop an appropriate conception of the meaning of the equal sign, they may revert to previous incorrect conceptions if they only see number sentences with the answer after the equal sign for an extended period of time.

Calculators may reinforce the notion that the equal sign means "carry out the preceding calculation" because they display an answer when the equal sign is pushed. It is doubtful, however, that children's misconceptions about the equal sign can be traced entirely to calculator use. Studies conducted before calculators were widely available found that children exhibited similar misconceptions about the equal sign.

A third possibility is that children may be predisposed to think of equality in terms of calculating answers rather than as a relation. Young children have an easier time carrying out a series of steps that lead to an answer than sorting out relations among quantities. However, the data summarized in Table 2.1 suggest that developing appropriate conceptions of the equal sign is not simply a matter of maturation. Unless we start to address directly children's concepts of equality, children's misconceptions will persist. On the other hand, we have found that children as young as first grade can learn the appropriate use of the equal sign. Furthermore, children's ability to understand the equal sign does not depend on their facility with computation. Children who are at relatively beginning stages in acquiring computational skills can still learn to use the equal sign appropriately. Developing an appropriate conception of the equal sign is something that we can and should work on for all children throughout the elementary grades.

CHILDREN'S CONCEPTIONS

The inappropriate generalizations about the equal sign that children make and often persist in defending are symptomatic of some fundamental limits in their understanding of how mathematical ideas are generated and justified. They have seen many examples of number sentences of a particular form, and they have overgeneralized from those examples. As they begin to justify conjectures about numbers and number relations, they tend to rely on examples and think that examples alone can prove their case. Thus, children's persistence in defending their conceptions of the meaning of the equal sign reflects their limited conceptions of how mathematical ideas are generated and justified.

It can be a challenge to get children to examine things that they believe to be true. Younger children, in particular, may have a difficult time considering several different ways of looking at equality and thinking about the consequences of the alternative perspectives. In general young children have difficulty in dealing with hypothetical situations and suspending judgment. But learning mathematics with understanding requires children to question why things work out the way that they do. As we shall see in the chapters to follow, children are more capable of reasoning and abstract thinking than they often have been given credit for. We need to appreciate the potential limits of children's thinking, but we do not want to impose limits on them because we do not anticipate what they are capable of. Time and again we have been surprised at what children can learn when we are attentive to what they are telling us.

CHALLENGES

1. What are the different responses that students may give to the following open number sentence: $9 + 7 = \square + 8$?
2. Why did Ms. L. ask Gina to solve the open number sentence $57 + 86 = \square + 84$ after she had solved the problem with smaller numbers? Are there any other questions you might have asked Gina or the other students described in this chapter to better understand their conceptions of the meaning of the equal sign and the relations between numerical expressions?
3. If you were the teacher in Teacher Commentary 2.2, what would you do next?
4. Design a sequence of true/false and/or open number sentences that you might use to engage your students in thinking about the equal sign. Describe why you selected the problems you did.
5. Discuss the problems you constructed for Challenge 4 with several students individually, a small group of students, or your class. Try to record or recall how specific students responded to the questions, what their responses suggested about their understanding of the meaning of the equal sign, and whether and how students' conceptions changed over the course of the discussion. Were there any critical features of the lesson that seemed to have the most significant effect in changing children's conceptions of the meaning of the equal sign?

REFERENCE

FALKNER, KAREN P., LEVI, LINDA, & CARPENTER, THOMAS P. 1999. "Children's Understanding of Equality: A Foundation for Algebra." *Teaching Children Mathematics* 6, 232–36.

3 | DEVELOPING AND USING RELATIONAL THINKING

In the last chapter we saw examples of two children (Ricardo and Gina) who understood that the equal sign represents a relation rather than a signal to carry out a calculation. Although both children used the equal sign correctly, their solutions to the problem $8 + 4 = \square + 5$ revealed important differences in their abilities to think about relations. To solve the problem, Ricardo actually carried out the calculation. He added 8 and 4 and then figured out what to add to 5 to get 12. Gina was more sophisticated in her thinking. She both recognized that the equal sign represented a relation between the answers to the calculations on each side of the equal sign and that she could look for relations between the two expressions on either side of the equal sign. She did not need to add $8 + 4$; she recognized that 5 was one more than 4, so the number in the box had to be one less than 8.

Ricardo's thinking represents an important milestone. He used the equal sign correctly. But he still considered the expressions on either side of the equal sign as calculations to carry out. Many students initially rely on solutions like Ricardo's as they begin to use the equal sign correctly. Other students, like Gina, quickly recognize that they do not always need to carry out the calculations; they can compare the expressions directly before they calculate. This is a critical advance over the type of thinking represented by Ricardo's solution. It allows students to express important relations such as

$$4 \times 7 = 7 + 7 + 7 + 7 \quad and \quad 37 \times 68 = 68 \times 37$$

A goal of this chapter is to consider how to engage all students in using this type of relational thinking. First we show how a second-grade student made the transition from computing to using relational thinking. In a second example, we show how one teacher constructed a series of number sentences to challenge her students to think about relations. In a third example, we illustrate how students can demonstrate their mathematical understanding as they write their own number sentences and as they discuss number sentences generated by the teacher to focus on particular mathematical ideas. The final major section of the chapter focuses on using number sentences as a tool to develop specific arithmetic concepts or skills. The specific example discussed in this chapter is the learning of number facts. Further examples appear in the Challenges section at the end of the chapter.

Emma Learns to Look for Relations

Emma is working through a series of problems with Ms. K. The first problem that Emma solves is 7 + 6 = ☐ + 5. She solves the problem by first calculating that 7 + 6 is equal to 13 and then figuring out what number can be added to 5 to get 13. At this point she shows no evidence of relational thinking. The numbers are relatively small, and it is easy for Emma to calculate. Ms. K. decides that as long as Emma can easily calculate, she will not be motivated to try to look for relations that will make it unnecessary to carry out the calculations. Therefore, Ms. K. gives Emma a problem that involves larger numbers: 43 + 28 = ☐ + 42. After a short pause, the following exchange takes place.

> **Emma:** I think it might, well, it's, those two equal 71.
>
> **Ms. K.:** How did you figure that out so quickly?
>
> **Emma:** I took the 40 and the 20 and added those and that was 60 and then 8, 9, 10, and there is one more and then you add one more ten onto the 60 and that is 70 and then there is one left, 71.

Although Emma is able to use quite sophisticated mental calculation to calculate 43 + 28, she needs to use base 10 blocks to figure out what to add to 42 to get 71. She does this successfully, but once again Emma does not take advantage of relations between the expressions 43 + 28 and ☐ + 42. She does not recognize that because 42 is 1 less than 43, the number in the box has to be 1 more than 28. Ms. K. asks Emma if there is an easier way that she could solve the problem and whether there is anything she notices about the numbers. Emma responds no to each question.

Ms. K. decides that Emma is going to continue to calculate for problems like the ones she has been solving, so she decides to try a problem in which the relation is more obvious:

> **Ms. K.:** What about this? [*Writes 15 + 16 = 15 +* ☐].
>
> **Emma:** [*Almost immediately*] Sixteen.
>
> **Ms. K.:** How did you do that so quickly?
>
> **Emma:** Because if it is 15 plus 16 equals 15 plus box, these are the same numbers [*points to the two 15s*] and these have to be the same numbers [*points to the 16 and the box*].

Next Ms. K. returns to a problem similar to those Emma has solved by calculating to see if Emma can now apply the same kind of thinking to this problem. The problem she gives is 28 + 32 = 27 + □. Emma looks at the problem for a long time and appears to be calculating in her head. Ms. K.'s goal is to help Emma see the relations that make it unnecessary to calculate, so she interrupts Emma's calculation.

Ms. K.: What are you thinking?

Emma: I was just, umm, adding up those two.
[*Indicating the 28 + 32*]

Ms. K.: I have a question. Do you remember how you did this one? [*Indicating 15 + 16 = 15 + □*]

Emma: Because if these two are the same numbers, since there are two numbers here and then it's the same number as before it has to be the same as that?

Ms. K.: Could you do something like that down there? [*Pointing to the new problem*]

Emma: Umm, no.

Emma then uses the blocks to figure out the sum of 28 and 32. She then starts to use the blocks to try to find what to add to 27 to get 60. Before she has completed solving the problem with the blocks, she hesitates and looks at the blocks. Ms. K. asks her what she is thinking.

FIGURE 3.1
Emma learns to think relationally.

Emma: I think it's 30 something.

Ms. K.: Why 30 something?

Emma: I think maybe 33.

Ms. K.: Why do you think that? That was pretty quick.

Emma: Because, I said 33 because 27 is one less than 28 and then 33 is one more than 32.

Ms. K.: Very interesting. Very good! I really like the way you did that. Let's try one more: $67 + 83 = \Box + 82$. What do you think?

Emma: I think it is 60 something.

Ms. K.: Okay, why do you think that?

Emma: Because, it is sort of like that one. [*Points to* $28 + 32 = 27 + \Box$]

Ms. K.: Oh, can you explain that to me?

Emma: Because this one [*points to 82*] is less than that one [*points to 83*], so it has to be less or more than that one.

Ms. K.: Okay, which do you think?

Emma: Umm, 68.

Ms. K.: Okay, why did you pick 68?

Emma: Because, I picked 68 because this one [82] is less than that one [83], and then I think it should be one more than this one [67]. Then it would be 68.

Ms. K.: You did a great job! What did you figure out when you were doing this?

Emma: I figured out just at these two last ones that all of these [*gestures to indicate all the other problems that she has done*] are sort of like the same, because this one [*pointing to the 6 in the first problem,* $7 + 6 = \Box + 5$] is more than this one [*pointing to the 5*] and this one [*pointing to the 7*] is less than that one [*pointing to the answer 8, which she has written in the box*].

A key transition in Emma's thinking occurs after Ms. K. asks her to solve $15 + 16 = 15 + \Box$. Emma immediately recognizes that she does not have to compute for this problem in which the numbers are the same, but she does not immediately recognize that she can use this type of thinking on the next problem and starts to compute again. Before she is done computing, however, she recognizes that she can figure out the answer to this problem without carrying out all the calculations. Emma then applies this type of thinking to the next problem and is able to recognize that she could have solved all the problems this way.

A Class Discussion of Number Sentences
Involving Relational Thinking

In the following classroom episode, Ms. F., a fourth-grade teacher, introduces true/false number sentences to her students at the beginning of the year. They have not yet talked about the equal sign, so Ms. F. presents only number sentences with a single number after the equal sign. Ms. F.'s goal is to familiarize her students with true/false number sentences before she uses them to engage students in a discussion of the equal sign. But she has a second goal: to encourage students to think flexibly about mathematical operations. She challenges them to think about how changes in the numbers being added or subtracted are reflected in the answer to the calculation.[1]

Ms. F.: Is this number sentence true or false?

$12 - 9 = 3$

Ms. F. starts with a relatively straightforward true number sentence.

Jamie: True.

Ms. F.: How do you know that's true?

Jamie: Because 12 minus 10 is 2, and 9 is one less, so the answer has to be one more.

Ms. F.: Did anybody figure it out a different way?

Students provide several different explanations how they know that $12 - 9$ is 3.

Ms. F.: How about this one?

$34 - 19 = 15$

Celia: True, because 34 take away 10 is 24, and take away 9 more is like take away 4 more and then 5 more, so it's 15.

Carrie: I think it's true, too. I did 34 take away 20. That's 14, but we only had to take away 19, so it's one more, 15, and that's what it says.

Students provide several additional explanations for how they know it is a true number sentence.

Ms. F.: How about this one?

$5 + 7 = 11$

James: False. Five and 7 is 12, not 11.

Ms. F.: Okay, how about this one?

$58 + 76 = 354$

Immediately a number of hands shoot up.

---

[1]The following episodes have been edited to focus on the critical exchanges about mathematical ideas.

Sarah: That's false.

Ms. F.:   How did you get that so quickly? You didn't have time to figure out 58 plus 76.

Sarah: I didn't have to. Fifty-eight and 78 are both less than 100, so the answer has to be less than 200.

Ms. F.:   How about this one?

$$27 + 48 - 48 = 27$$

Rachael: That's true, because you just add the 48 and then take the same thing away again, so it's just the 27 you started with.

Rachael: See, you have the 27 here. [*Points to a collection of 2 ten blocks and 7 units*] And you add 48. [*Using tens and ones, she represents 48 and moves them next to the blocks representing 27, but she keeps the piles separate so the 27 and the 48 are in distinct piles.*] Then you just take away these same 48. [*She removes the set of 48.*] And you are left with the 27 you started with. So it's 27.

Ms. F.:   Let's try another one.

$$345 + 568 - 568 = 353$$

Carlos: That's false. It's just like the other one. The answer should be 345, not 353.

Ms. F.:   How about this? Can you do this without doing all the adding and subtracting?

$$48 + 63 - 62 = 49$$

Jana: The numbers aren't the same like last time, so we have to figure it out.

Sarah: They're not the same, but they are almost the same. You add 63 and take away 62. That's like adding 1. So it is true.

This problem establishes that students do not necessarily have to calculate to decide if a number sentence is true or false.

Some students set about calculating 27 + 48, but several raise their hands almost immediately. Without waiting for the students to finish their calculations, Ms. F. calls on Rachael, who has her hand up.

The class discusses Rachael's explanation. Some students are not convinced, so Ms. F. gets out base ten blocks for Rachael to use to show what she was thinking.

Ms. F. selects a problem that extends the idea that they have been using in the previous problems. This extension is relatively transparent because the numbers are close, so the required calculation (63 − 62) is quite simple.

Ms. F.:   Here's another.

$674 + 56 - 59 = 671$

This is slightly more complicated than the preceding problem because students have to recognize that they can subtract 56 from the 56 given in the problem, but then they have to subtract 3 more from 674. This is quite different from the problem in which they could simply subtract one number from the number they added.

Raymond: Yeah. That's true. You're taking away three more than you added, so the answer has to be three less.

Later in the year after students have learned that the equal sign expresses a relation, Ms. F. revisits these ideas. In these problems, students are asked to think about numerical expressions as something more than a series of calculations. They are asked to use properties of numbers and operations to think about relations between numerical expressions.[2]

Ms. F.:   Today we're going to look at some open number sentences. What number does c have to be to make this number sentence true?

$12 + 9 = 10 + 8 + c$

Ms. F. starts with a relatively easy example involving adding relatively small numbers.

Sarah: Twelve and 9 is 21 and 10 and 8 is 18, so you have to put 3 more with the 18 to get 21. So c is 3.

With these small numbers, students can simply compute to figure out the answer.

Almost all students raise their hands.

Ms. F.:   How many think c is 3? Okay, did anybody figure it out a different way?

Carlos: I did. I saw that 12 is two more than 10, and 9 is one more than 8. So you have to add 3.

---

[2]In Chapter 2, we consistently used a box to represent an unknown in an open number sentence. The box has the appearance of a space that can be filled in with a number, and it often is presumed to be easier for children to relate to putting a number in the box than replacing a letter with a number. The basic question we are asking, however, is: "What number can we replace the box with to make the number sentence true?" We generally start with a box when introducing open number sentences to young children, but we have found that they quite readily adapt to using letters to represent variables and unknowns. In the remainder of this chapter and in subsequent chapters, we use letters to denote variables and unknowns.

Ms. F.: Does everybody understand Carlos's way? Okay, here's another one.

$$345 + 576 = 342 + 574 + d$$

There is a general nodding of assent.

Ms. F. picks a problem that has much larger numbers but the same general structure. The operation is addition and both numbers on the right of the equal sign are smaller than the corresponding numbers on the left. Ms. F. presumes that the larger numbers will discourage students from simply computing as Sarah did.

Rachael: It's 5. See, 342 is three less and 574 is two less, so you have to put 5 more on to make it come out the same.

Sam: I did it a different way. There's 300 on each side, so I took them off, and you can do the same thing with the 500s. That gave me 45 plus 76 equals 42 plus 74 plus *d*. Now you can do the same thing again with the 40s and the 70s, and that leaves 5 plus 6 equals 2 plus 4 plus *d*. And that's 11 and 6, so *d* has to be 5 to make that side 11.

There is some discussion of this strategy and how it is the same as Carlos's strategy on the previous problem.

Ms. F. had not anticipated this answer. It is quite different from Carlos and Rachael's strategy, but it involves an important mathematical idea that Sam later states in response to a question from Ms. F.

Ms. F.: Does everybody understand what Sam did? Sam, maybe you should explain it again.

Sam explains again and responds to several students' questions.

Ms. F.: Sam, how do you know that you can do that?

Sam: If something is the same on both sides of the equal sign, you don't even have to think about it, you can just get rid of it. When you get rid of what's the same, the numbers get smaller and then it gets real easy to tell what *d* is equal to.

Sam states a general rule to justify his response, but he does not address the question of how he knows that the rule is valid. Ms. F. pursues the discussion a little further and then moves on to another problem.

Ms. F.: Can you always do that? Can you subtract any number like that?

Sam: Yes.

Two days later, Ms. F. poses the following problem:

$$46 + 28 = 27 + 50 - p$$

This problem differs from the problems the students had been solving in several ways. One of the numbers on the right of the equation has been increased, and one has been decreased. The order of the numbers also has been changed.

Sarah: The 27 is one less, and the 50 is four more. So you have to subtract 3.

Ms. F.: The 27 is one less than what?

Sarah: One less than the 28, and the 50 is four more than the 46.

About a week later, Ms. F. poses the following problem:

$$82 - 28 = 86 - 29 - g$$

Ms. F. asks Sarah to be more precise in explaining her response.

By this point most students seem to have figured out how to deal with addition problems, so Ms. F. moves on to subtraction. Because the students have been relatively successful with the addition problems she has posed, she starts off with a subtraction problem in which both numbers change. The students need a little longer to work on this problem before sharing their solutions.

Rich: It's 5. You made it four more and one more. So that's 5 you have to take away.

Jana: That's not the way it works on this one. The 86 is four more than 82, but you're taking away more too with the 29. You need to take that one away from the 4, so g is 3, not 5.

Since this is a complicated problem, Ms. F. spends a good deal of time getting Jana and others to clarify this strategy. Many children have questions for Jana. Even after much discussion there are some children who do not yet understand this strategy and revert to solving both sides to figure the value of g.

There are a number of critical features of Ms. F.'s instruction in these episodes. In these interactions, we see class norms that have been established in the class: students explain their thinking, they listen to one another, and alternative strategies for solving a given problem are valued and discussed. Ms. F. also is working on establishing a norm that solutions that involve more than simply calculating answers are not only accepted but valued. The sequences of problems that Ms. F. selected were appropriate for her class. She started with relatively easy problems and selected problems that provided an appropriate level of challenge based on what she had observed the students doing on previous problems. This does not mean that the same sequences would be appropriate for any class, or for that matter, for any fourth-grade class. Ms. F. selected problems that she knew would challenge her students but would not be too difficult for them, and she made decisions about what problems to use next based on students' responses to problems that they had already solved.

In these exchanges we also observe some interesting student responses. In solving the subtraction problem near the end of the last class, Rich tried to generalize a procedure that was successful for addition problems but failed to take into account that the strategy needs to be modified to apply to subtraction problems. Earlier, Sam used an interesting strategy for relating sums of large numbers that showed insight into an important principle. Subtracting the same number from both sides of an equation is used frequently in solving algebra equations. In fact, it also is possible to add the same number to both sides of an equation and to multiply or divide each side of an equation by the same number. The principles underlying these transformations are discussed in Chapter 9.

Another Context for Engaging Students with Relational Thinking

Another way that number sentences can provide a context for students to engage with relations involving important mathematical ideas is by having them write true/false number sentences themselves. We have found that students are intrigued and motivated by writing true/false number sentences, and writing number sentences that involve a lot of numbers but require little difficult computation is particularly intriguing. The number sentences that students write also provide a good window on their understanding of and inclination to think about relations and use basic mathematical ideas. Furthermore, students frequently write more interesting number sentences than we would write, and sharing the number sentences that they write can result in stimulating and productive discussions of mathematical ideas.

Following are some examples of true/false number sentences generated by one third-grade student. The work of six additional students appears in the exercises at the end of the chapter. In giving the assignment, the teacher challenged the students to write some number sentences that involved more than computation.

In response to this challenge, Cody wrote the true/false number sentences that appear in Figure 3.2. The first group of number sentences shows potential understanding of a number of important mathematical ideas. In each of these number sentences, he used the zero property of addition $(10 + 0 = 10)$. He also used multiples of ten to make his calculation relatively easy. In the second and third number sentences, he also used the idea that if you subtract a number from itself, the answer is zero $(100 - 100 = 0)$. All of the number sentences in the next group are false. He thought he might fool people with these problems, because $90 - 100$ is not equal to 10. In the final group of number sentences, he changed the order in which the numbers were added $(24 + 47 = 47 + 24)$, illustrating another fundamental idea of arithmetic. None of Cody's number sentences requires difficult computation, but they all provide an interesting challenge, because they make use of fundamental ideas of arithmetic to avoid or simplify the computation.

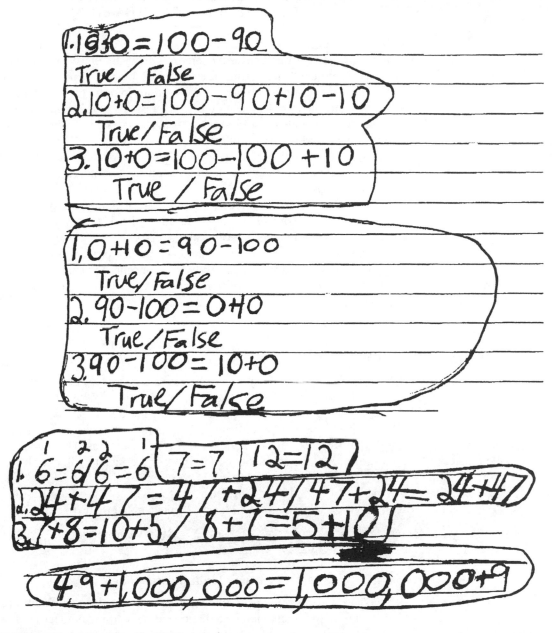

1. 1930 = 100 − 90

    True / False

2. 10 + 0 = 100 − 90 + 10 − 10

    True / False

3. 10 + 0 = 100 − 100 + 10

    True / False

1. 0 + 0 = 90 − 100

    True / False

2. 90 − 100 = 0 + 0

    True / False

3. 90 − 100 = 10 + 0

    True / False

1. 6 = 6 / 6 = 6 / 7 = 7 / 12 = 12

2. 24 + 47 = 47 + 24 / 47 + 24 = 24 + 47

3. 7 + 8 = 10 + 5 / 8 + 7 = 5 + 10

4. 9 + 1,000,000 = 1,000,000 + 9

FIGURE 3.2   *Cody's True/False Number Sentences*

USING RELATIONAL THINKING TO SUPPORT
THE LEARNING OF ARITHMETIC

Many fundamental mathematical ideas involve relations between different representations of numbers and operations on them. Once students begin to think about relations, true/false and open number sentences provide flexible contexts for representing these relations in order to draw children's attention to them and for children to express their own understanding. These number sentences can provide specific contexts for children to talk about their understanding of basic mathematical ideas. Class or small-group discussions of appropriately selected number sentences can provide a basis to lift out these big ideas for discussion and examination by all members of the class.

The development of students' mathematical thinking should not be perceived as one more topic to teach. Ideally, it should be an integral part of the teaching of arithmetic concepts and skills. Once students have learned to think about relations, true/false and open number sentences can be used to support the learning of many arithmetic concepts and skills. One example is discussed in the next section. Others appear in the challenges at the end of the chapter.

TEACHER COMMENTARY 3.1

When I first started doing algebra, I really didn't know where it would go in my class. I would think, "I am going to focus on algebra today and try out some of these ideas." After using these ideas throughout the year, I started seeing what my kids could do and how this algebra work could be embedded in all that we do with arithmetic. Our team looked at the NCTM Standards and talked about what kinds of things we do to address the Standards. The big ideas about algebra really fit into each of the standards we teach. I ask the kids to talk and think about how things work as they do. Math is more than just procedures; I really want to help kids from doing math in a rote way. I want them to understand. It is really important that this algebra piece isn't seen as just one more thing to add. It really fits with all we do in math.

Barb Wiesner, First-grade teacher

Learning Multiplication Facts

True/false and open number sentences can be used to draw children's attention to relations among numbers that can make learning number facts easier. Knowing that multiplication is commutative reduces the quantity of number facts that children have to learn by almost one-half. Understanding the relation between addition and multiplication makes it possible for students to relate the learning of multiplication facts to their knowledge of addition. Focusing on specific relationships among multiplication facts can

make it possible for students to build on the facts they have learned.
Following are some examples of true/false number sentences that draw upon these relations. The first three examples illustrate the relation between addition and multiplication. The relation between addition and multiplication is particularly useful for students when initially learning number facts involving 3 and 4. These examples of true/false number sentences can be used to engage students in a discussion of this relation.[3]

> a. $3 \times 7 = 7 + 7 + 7$
> b. $3 \times 7 = 14 + 7$
> c. $4 \times 6 = 12 + 12$

The next five examples illustrate the relations among number facts. Children tend to learn some number facts earlier than others. For some numbers, such as 2, 5, and 9, there are patterns that make learning the number facts easier. More difficult facts can be related to facts that students already have learned.

> d. $3 \times 8 = 2 \times 8 + 8$
> e. $6 \times 7 = 5 \times 7 + 7$
> f. $8 \times 6 = 8 \times 5 + 6$*
> g. $7 \times 6 = 7 \times 5 + 7$
> h. $9 \times 7 = 10 \times 7 - 7$

Students may solve these problems initially by actually carrying out the calculations on each side of the equal sign. That is all right as a beginning, but the goal is to help students recognize that the expressions on each side of the equal sign represent the same number without having to calculate. If students already have some experience looking for relations between expressions, they may be more likely to focus on these relations rather than carry out the calculations. The goal is to build on students' ability to consider relations between expressions to help them focus on the principles relating multiplication and addition. It may take time for students to develop this understanding, but it can pay big dividends in the long run by making learning meaningful.

TEACHER COMMENTARY 3.2

Many children miss the big ideas when they work through the curriculum in a procedural way. For example, I am thinking about three fourth graders who still didn't know their subtraction facts. I watched them work through a sheet of facts. One student was counting backward by ones. She was overwhelmed, and she wasn't using any big ideas. I talked with the three students and asked them, "Can you think of some tricky, shortcut ways to do some of these facts?"

[3]An asterisk (*) denotes a false number sentence.

One student said, "If you have 4 plus 4 equals 8, then 8 minus 4 equals 4." This is a big idea, a big algebraic idea.

I told the students, "Let's go through each of these facts and find something neat." We did, and for every fact we found something neat.

Like for 15 − 8, one student said, "Well, 16 minus 8 equals 8, so 15 minus 8 equals 7." Another student said, "I would do 15 minus 8 like this, 15 minus 5 is 10 and then minus 3 more is 7." A while ago, I would have seen this just as breaking numbers apart, but really this is a big idea in algebra. Symbolically, she was doing $a − (b + c) = (a − b) − c$.

By looking at the strategies that involve these big ideas, these students' whole approach to learning facts has changed. The student who counted back by ones wasn't doing that anymore; she was thinking about each number fact and what big idea she could apply. Memorization didn't work for any of these children. Soon these kids will be efficient with their subtraction facts and at the same time know some important mathematics. I want kids to know that math is about understanding and I want them to want to understand. Algebraic thinking should be the foundation for building a child's mathematical knowledge and for building your mathematics curriculum. If you are doing stuff that doesn't tie into these big ideas, you are wasting precious time.

Carrie Valentine, Teacher, Grades 3–6

THINKING RELATIONALLY

The kind of student engagement that we have described in this chapter is important for two reasons. First, it can facilitate children's learning of arithmetic. We have tried to portray that algebraic reasoning is not a separate topic; it is integrally bound with learning arithmetic, and it can make the learning of arithmetic easier and richer. Second, it provides a foundation for smoothing the transition to algebra. When students traditionally learn arithmetic, they think about adding, subtracting, multiplying, and dividing entirely as procedures to be carried out. That conception is one of the things that leads them to conclude that the equal sign must always be followed by the answer to a given calculation. It also gets in the way of their learning algebra. In algebra, students must deal with expressions that involve adding, subtracting, multiplying, and dividing but that are not amenable to calculation (e.g., $3x + 7y − 4z$). They have to think about relations between expressions ($5x + 34 = 79 − 2x$) as they attempt to figure out how to transform equations in order to solve them. The kinds of thinking that students are challenged to do with the types of problems discussed in this chapter pave the way for the thinking that is required to deal with these and other problems that students will encounter.

CHALLENGES

1. The following number sentences might encourage relational thinking. In these examples, larger numbers are used to discourage calculation. Describe how students might use relational thinking to respond to these number sentences. Note that not all of the number sentences are true.

    a. $37 + 56 = 39 + 54$
    b. $33 - 27 = 34 - 26$
    c. $471 - 382 = 474 - 385$
    d. $674 - 389 = 664 - 379$
    e. $583 - 529 = 83 - 29$
    f. $37 \times 54 = 38 \times 53$
    g. $60 \times 48 = 6 \times 480$
    h. $5 \times 84 = 10 \times 42$
    i. $64 \div 14 = 32 \div 28$
    j. $42 \div 16 = 84 \div 32$
    k. $67 - 49 = c - 46$
    l. $234 + 578 = 234 + 576 + d$
    m. $94 + 87 - 38 = 94 + 85 - 39 + f$

2. Rank the following problems from easiest to most difficult:

    a. $73 + 56 = 71 + d$
    b. $92 - 57 = g - 56$
    c. $68 + b = 57 + 69$
    d. $56 - 23 = f - 25$
    e. $96 + 67 = 67 + p$
    f. $87 + 45 = y + 46$
    g. $74 - 37 = 75 - q$

3. Rank the following problems from easiest to most difficult:

    a. $73 + 56 = 71 + 59 - d$
    b. $92 - 57 = 94 - 56 + g$
    c. $68 + 58 = 57 + 69 - b$
    d. $56 - 23 = 59 - 25 - s$
    e. $96 + 67 = 67 + 93 + p$
    f. $87 + 45 = 86 + 46 + t$
    g. $74 - 37 = 71 - 39 + q$

4. Look at Sam's solution in the discussion of students' solutions in Ms. F's class. Could he use the same strategy to solve the following problem?

    $573 - 368 = 571 - 364 - t$

5. Write a series of problems that you might use with your students to encourage them to begin to look for relations. Be prepared to discuss why you selected the problems you did. Consider how you might modify the sequence of problems depending on students' responses.

6. Discuss the problems with your class or a group of students in your class. Describe the key interactions that illustrate your students' abilities to consider relations. Which problems were particularly fruitful in encouraging students to think about relations?

7. Reflecting on the interview with Emma in this chapter, what problems do you think she could solve without difficulty, and what problems might be appropriate to challenge Emma to further develop her use of relational thinking? Which of the problems in Challenge 1 do you think that she might be able to solve using relational thinking, and which would be too difficult for her?

8. Can you think of other true/false number sentences that students might figure out without carrying out the complete calculation?

9. **Developing addition number facts.** True/false and open number sentences also can be used to draw children's attention to relations among numbers that can make learning addition facts easier. Knowing that addition is commutative reduces the number of number facts that children have to learn by almost half. Focusing on specific relationships among number facts also can make the learning of number facts easier. Children tend to learn some addition number facts before others, and they naturally use these known facts to generate closely related combinations. Children tend to learn doubles (6 + 6, 9 + 9) before most other number facts, and they use these known facts to generate the answer to facts that are one or two greater or less than a double. Facts involving 9 also are relatively easy to learn if children have some beginning understanding of base ten numbers. True/false and open number sentences provide a context to help children focus on these relations. Write a series of true/false number sentences that might illustrate specific relations among number facts to engage students in a discussion of them.

10. **Developing base ten concepts.** True/false and open number sentences also can be used to focus on features of base ten numbers, as illustrated by the following examples. Some of the examples are quite elementary; others get at more subtle issues. One of the possibilities with true/false number sentences is to include common errors as false number sentences to make the errors a focus for discussion. Which of the following problems do you think would provide an interesting challenge to your students? Why? How do you think they would justify their answers? Note that not all of the number sentences are true.

    a. 56 = 50 + 6
    b. 87 = 7 + 80
    c. 93 = 9 + 30

   d. 94 = 80 + 14
   e. 94 = 70 + 24
   f. 246 = 24 × 10 + 6
   g. 86 = 6 + *f*
   h. 240 = 24 × *k*
   i. 47 + 38 = 40 + 30 + 7 + 8
   j. 24 + 78 = 78 + 20 + 2 + 2
   k. 63 - 28 = 60 – 20 –3 – 8
   l. 63 - 28 = 60 – 20 + 3 – 8
   m. 0.78 = .078
   n. 1.95 = 1.9500

11. Can you write some additional problems that might challenge your students to think about place value ideas?

12. Figures 3.3 through 3.6 show some examples of student-generated number sentences. What do you think each of the examples suggests about the student's understanding of mathematics? What specific big ideas of mathematics do you think these examples illustrate? Which examples do you think might be particularly productive to discuss?

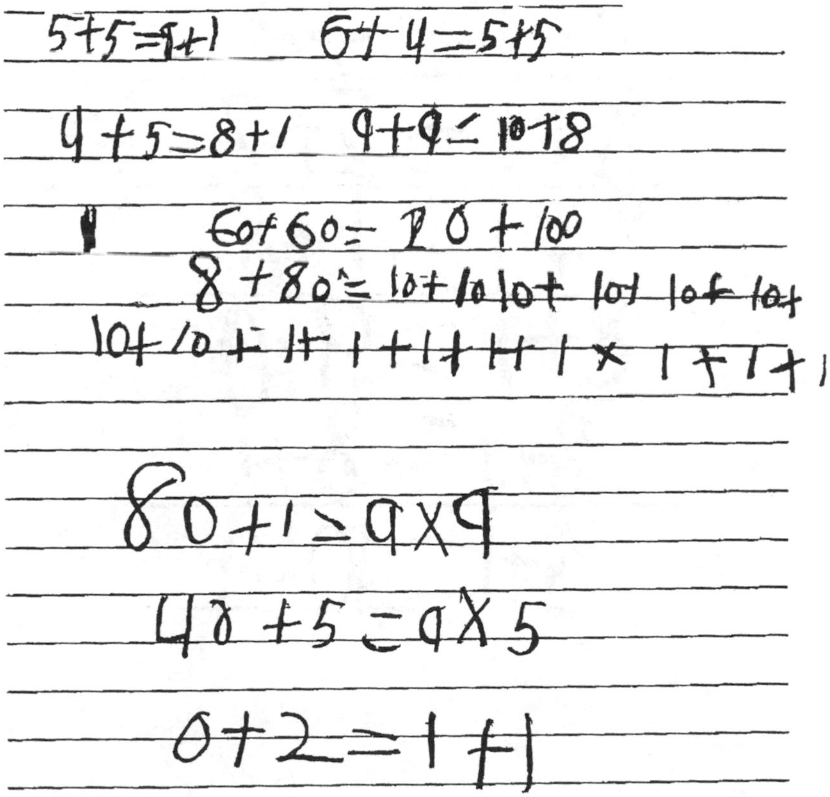

FIGURE 3.3
Kevin's Work

FIGURE 3.4   *Ahren's Work*

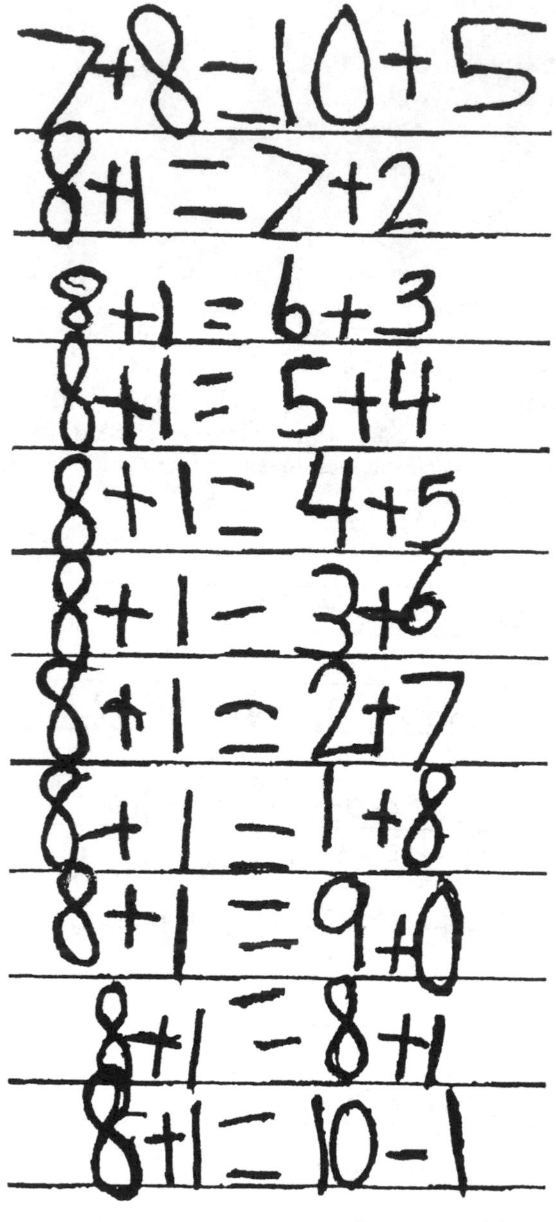

$$7+8=10+5$$
$$8+1=7+2$$
$$8+1=6+3$$
$$8+1=5+4$$
$$8+1=4+5$$
$$8+1=3+6$$
$$8+1=2+7$$
$$8+1=1+8$$
$$8+1=9+0$$
$$8+1=8+1$$
$$8+1=10-1$$

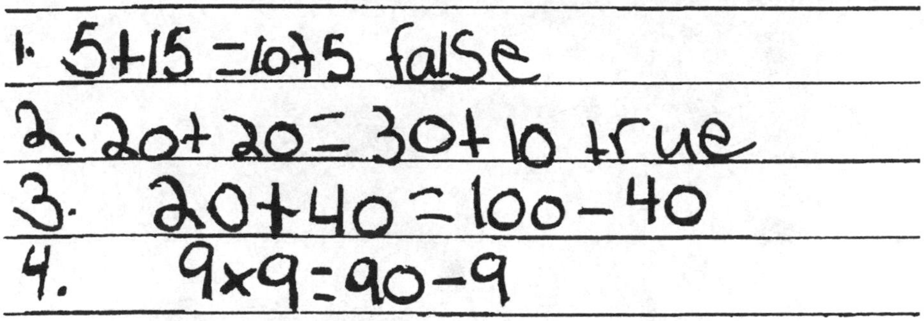

1. $5+15 = 1075$ false
2. $20+20 = 30+10$ true
3. $20+40 = 100-40$
4. $9 \times 9 = 90-9$

FIGURE 3.5 *Lesley's Work*

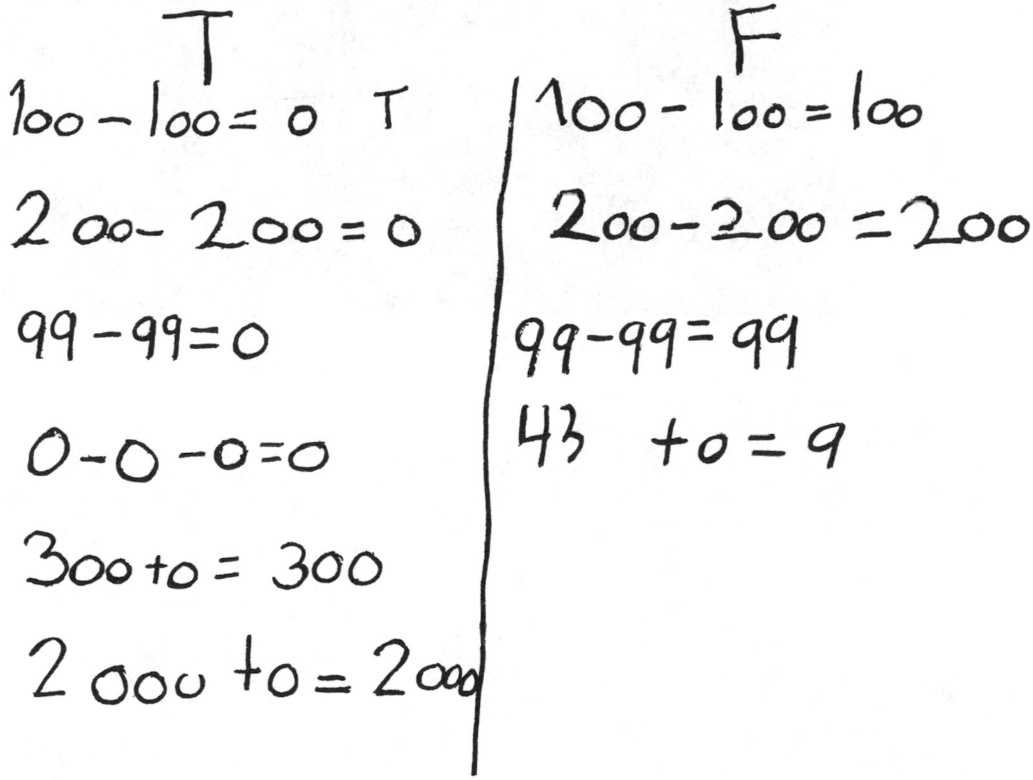

T

$100-100 = 0$ T

$200-200 = 0$

$99-99 = 0$

$0-0-0 = 0$

$300+0 = 300$

$2000+0 = 2000$

F

$100-100 = 100$

$200-200 = 200$

$99-99 = 99$

$43 \quad +0 = 9$

FIGURE 3.6 *Eve's Work*

4 | MAKING CONJECTURES ABOUT MATHEMATICS

In Chapter 3, we considered examples of how true/false and open number sentences could provide a context for children to focus on mathematical relations in learning mathematics concepts and skills. In this chapter we want to push that idea a little further. Children have a great deal of implicit knowledge about fundamental properties in mathematics, but it usually is not a regular part of mathematics class to make that knowledge explicit. Most children know, for example, that when they add zero to a number the sum is the number they started with ($a + 0 = a$ is a true number sentence for any substitution for a). In fact, most children know a lot of things about zero ($a - 0 = a$, $a - a = 0$, $a \times 0 = 0$). They also have some implicit knowledge about being able to change the order of numbers when they add them ($a + b = b + a$). But children do not often have an opportunity to articulate and examine these ideas. When they do, we sometimes discover that they are not sure that the principles they work with are true for all numbers. They may, for example, readily change the order of small numbers when they add them, but not be sure that they can change the order when the numbers are very large. This becomes critical when they start manipulating algebraic expressions and have to apply these principles to expressions that contain variables as well as numbers. At that point they have to have an explicit understanding of the principles, or the manipulations they perform on algebraic expressions become meaningless procedures.

MAKING IMPLICIT KNOWLEDGE EXPLICIT

In this chapter we consider how to engage elementary school children in making conjectures about mathematical ideas to make their informal knowledge about properties of number operations explicit. There are two issues related to this theme that we address in this chapter:

- considering how students articulate, refine, and edit their conjectures, and
- identifying important mathematical ideas for students to make conjectures about.

TEACHER COMMENTARY 4.1

I like to have conversations with my kids about math, but sometimes the conversations can get all over the place. When this happens, I always have a lot of kids who do not participate; a lot of kids cannot even follow the conversation because it is just too much. What I like about the conjectures is that the discussion becomes a focused beam of conversation. Everyone is pulled in since we are concentrated on one big idea, like switching the numbers around when you multiply. It is much easier than many other conversations I have tried about number. Even my student who has the most trouble attending can attend. I really believe that they learn from defending their ideas and questioning others' ideas. You need to have a way to talk about math. Conjectures are a way to talk about big ideas that all my kids participate in.

Nancy Lanyon, Fourth- and fifth-grade teacher

ARTICULATING, REFINING, AND EDITING CONJECTURES

Our goal in focusing on how students articulate, refine, and edit conjectures goes beyond simply engaging students in communicating about mathematics. It is important that students understand the necessity of using precise language in stating mathematical ideas, but in addition, we have found that in the process of carefully articulating, refining, and editing conjectures, students confront important mathematical ideas and engage in basic forms of mathematical argument. As illustrated in the following interaction, students are engaged in fundamental mathematical thinking as they are constructing conjectures.

We have found that true/false number sentences provide an ideal context for beginning to get children to articulate basic mathematical principles. The properties that often are easiest for children to identify and articulate involve operations with zero. Many children can quite readily identify these properties and state them accurately. Consider, for example, the following interaction in a small group of students in a second-grade class:

> **Mr. C.:** How about this number sentence? [*Writes 58 + 0 = 58 on the board*] Is it true or false?
>
> **Children:** True. True.

Rather than immediately pressing the children to make a generalization, Mr. C. gives them another number sentence illustrating the same principle, but in this case the number sentence is false.

> **Mr. C.:** How about this one? [*Writes 78 + 49 = 78*]
>
> **Children:** False! No, no false! No way!
>
> **Mr. C.:** Why is that false?

Jenny:	Because it's the same number as in the beginning, and you already put more with it, so it would have to be higher than the number you started with.
Mike:	Unless it was 78 plus zero equals 78. That would be right.
Mr. C.:	Why is that true? We added something.
Steve:	But that something is, like, nothing. Zero is nothing.
Mr. C.:	Is that always going to work?
Lynn:	If you want to start with a number and end with a number, and you do a number sentence, you should always put a zero. Since you wrote 78 plus 49 equals 78, you have to change a 49 to zero to equal 78, because if you want the same answer as the first number and the last number, you have to make a zero in between.
Mr. C.:	So do you think that will always work with zero? How about this one? [*Writes 789,564 + 0 = 789,564*]
Children:	That's true.
Mr. C.:	How do you know that is true? Have you ever done that? Ann?
Ann:	I will tell you. All those numbers plus zero, you won't add anything, so it would be the same number.
Mr. C.:	So we kind of have a rule here, don't we? What's the rule?
Ann:	Anything with a zero can be the right answer.
Mike:	No. Because if it was 100 plus 100, that's 200.
Jenny:	That's not what we are talking about. It doesn't have just plain zero.
Ann:	I said, umm, if you have a zero in it, it can't be like 100, because you want just plain zero, like 0 plus 7 equals 7.

After some additional discussion to clarify that the children are talking about the number zero, not zero in numbers like 20 or 500, the children are challenged to state a rule that they could share with the rest of the class.

Ellen:	When you put zero with one other number, just one zero with the other number, it equals the other number.
Steve:	Not true.
Mr. C.:	Wait. Let me make sure I got it. You said, "If you have a plain zero with another number." With another number? Like just sitting next to the number?
Ellen:	No, added with another number, it equals that number.
Mr. C.:	Okay. So what do we want to say here? Ann.
Ann:	Zero added with another number equals that other number.
Mr. C.:	Is that always going to be true for any number, even really big numbers that we haven't tried?
Children:	Yes. Yes.
Mr. C.:	How do you know that? Ellen.

Ellen:	Because zero is nothing. You're not putting anything with the number, so it is still the same.
Mr. C.:	Do you all agree?
Children:	Yes.
Mr. C.:	So we have a *conjecture* here about adding zero to any number. Can anybody think of another different conjecture about zero that is true for all numbers?
Lynn:	I can. You can take away zero from a number, and you get that number back.
Mr. C.:	Is that always going to be true for every number?
Children:	Yes.
Mr. C.:	How do you know? Steve.
Steve:	Because, it's just like the last one only it's take away. You're not taking anything away.
Mr. C.:	We should write these conjectures down so we can remember them and so we can share them with the rest of the class.

Mr. C. writes each conjecture on a separate sheet of paper.

> *Zero added with another number equals that number.*
> *You can take away zero from a number, and you get that number back.*

The conjectures are shared with the rest of the class, and the sheets are put up on the wall. The next day the class is working on some additional true/false number sentences. Note that Mr. C. introduced the term conjecture *by using it in context.*

Mr. C.:	How about this one, is this true or false? [*Writes 785 – 785 = 0 on the board*]
Class:	True. True.
Mr. C.:	Those are pretty big numbers. Are you sure?
Sally:	Yeah. Whenever you take a number away from itself, you get zero.
Ann:	[*Excitedly*] Hey, we have another conjecture here. A number minus the same number is zero.
Mr. C.:	Are you sure that's always true? How do you know?
Carla:	If you have some things and you take them all away, there's none left. It's zero.

Mr. C. writes this conjecture (*A number minus the same number is zero*) on another sheet of paper and adds it to the two conjectures already posted on the wall. Throughout the rest of the year, students continue to add to the list of conjectures. Some of the conjectures are motivated by true/false and open number sentences like these examples, others are suggested spontaneously by students as they notice some property of numbers that they think is always true. In this way, generating conjectures becomes a norm of the class.

In these examples, children readily applied properties of zero to determine whether number sentences were true or false. They both applied the properties to solve given problems involving zeros and justified their solutions by actually stating properties they were using. In this way their implicit knowledge about adding zero became explicit. Mr. C. used the children's explanations to encourage them to reflect on these properties and to state them precisely.

Ellen's initial statement of the zero property was not accurate, but collectively the students identified the limitations and constructed a more specific, valid statement of the property. This frequently occurs as children attempt to articulate a conjecture. The language often is not very precise, and the conjectures need to be edited to make them accurate. In this example, the students themselves recognized the ambiguity of the initial statements of the conjectures, and they proposed counterexamples to show that the statement of the conjecture was not true. For example, Mike challenged Ann's conjecture that "Anything with a zero can be the right answer" with the counterexample 100 + 100 = 200. That forced Ann to revise her assertion to make it more precise.

Students can be encouraged to edit the conjectures to provide precise language. Using counterexamples to show that a statement is not correct and needs to be revised is an important form of mathematical reasoning. In this example, the students themselves spontaneously adopted that form of argument, but sometimes it is necessary for the teacher to model this behavior for students. An ultimate goal is for students to recognize the value of this form of argument and use it in challenging the validity of conjectures or the ways that conjectures are stated. When conjectures are not stated precisely, counterexamples usually can be found that meet the conditions of the stated conjecture but clearly violate the conclusion of the conjecture.

TEACHER COMMENTARY 4.2

When I teach, I make instruction as language-rich as possible. This includes mathematics instruction. I think we limit children's experiences when we view language and mathematics as separate endeavors. Our current culture can also limit children's language growth, as today's media often replaces language with visual images. Kids struggling with language need to engage in, not be excused from, language-intensive experiences in all content areas. Many kids might need some support when engaging in language-rich math experiences. I support language learning by remembering to pair my words with a gesture or image. I watch for students' subtle signs that indicate confusion and rephrase my words. I make it a habit to ask students to use their own words to restate a classmate's idea. Classroom communities must value questions as positive interactions. It is true that language can interfere with learning, but language can also nurture learning.

Margaret Jensen, Teacher, Grades 1–3

Editing Conjectures

Students sometimes initially will describe a conjecture with one or several examples, as illustrated by the following exchange that leads to a conjecture about the commutative property of multiplication:

David: You know, it's like 7 times 5 equals 5 times 7, and 38 times 49 equals 49 times 38.

Ms. B.:   Can someone state that as a conjecture? Tyquelia?

Tyquelia: When you multiply numbers, you can change them around.

Ms. B.:   What does everybody think about that? Maybe we should write it down, so everybody can see it. [*Tyquelia writes the conjecture on the board.*] So what do you think?

There is a general nodding of heads. Not everyone seems quite sure.

Sarah: What about this? [*Goes to the board and writes* $49 \times 25 = 52 \times 94$]

Tyquelia: No, that's not what I mean.

Sarah: But didn't I just change the numbers around?

Tyquelia: I mean the numbers you multiply.

Ms. B.:   Perhaps we can state the conjecture in language so that it clearly doesn't allow the kind of thing that Sarah did. Would someone like to edit the conjecture for us?

Paul: How about this? When you multiply two numbers, you can change the order of the two numbers you are multiplying.

The students in this class collectively propose and refine conjectures. If there is disagreement, students often provide a specific example to illustrate why a conjecture needs to be stated more clearly. In this example, Ms. B. chose to ignore the fact that Sarah did not really change the order of the numbers; she changed the order of the digits in the numbers so that she generated new numbers. The statement of the conjecture seemed ambiguous for at least some of the class, so they decided it should be edited.

TEACHER COMMENTARY 4.3

It is great when kids make a conjecture. We write it down and hang it in the room, but that is only the beginning of the discussion. We continually puzzle through some of these big ideas: "Do we know that these big ideas will always work?" "How will this big idea help you?" "Why is it important for us to think about this?" I do this kind of thinking with the kids in my class. For example, I might ask, "Why would knowing that you can switch the order of numbers to add help you to do math?" "Can you think of when that might help you?" "How is it going to help you with your arithmetic?" We keep talking about how this all comes together. Putting the conjecture on the wall is not the end of the discussion.

Annie Keith, Second- and third-grade teacher

SOME CONJECTURES ABOUT BASIC PROPERTIES OF NUMBER OPERATIONS

The goal in engaging students in making conjectures is more than simply getting students to talk about mathematics and make mathematical ideas explicit. We want students to make conjectures not just for the sake of making conjectures, but because the ideas that they make conjectures about are important mathematical ideas that provide them power to learn new mathematics, to solve problems, and to understand the mathematics they are learning and using. As a consequence, we need to think carefully about the kinds of mathematical principles that it is most important for students to make conjectures about.

Table 4.1 shows a list of some of the basic properties of number operations. In a later chapter we will discuss some additional properties of number operations that are a little more difficult for children. We state each property in language children might use and as an open number sentence that is always true for all numbers. In a later chapter, we will talk more about writing conjectures using open number sentences. Initially, children usually write conjectures in natural language as in Table 4.1. We also provide examples of some true/false and open number sentences that are likely to elicit the conjectures. Note that many of the true/false and open number sentences include relatively large numbers. We have found that larger numbers frequently are more effective in drawing out children's conjectures about properties of number operations. The children are less likely to simply say that they did the computation, and their justifications for their answer often involve stating a conjecture.

Note that Conjectures 1, 4, and 7 have two similar statements. The only difference between them is that the order of the numbers is reversed. Once one of these conjectures has been established, the other follows from it. For example, if we know that $a + 0 = a$, then it follows that $0 + a = a$ also, because addition is commutative.

The conjectures in Table 4.1 are related in interesting and important ways. Conjectures involving addition and subtraction with zero often are the first conjectures that students make, and once they have made one of the conjectures, they frequently quite easily think of the related conjectures involving zero. There are important parallels between the conjectures involving addition and subtraction with zero and multiplication and division with 1. Essentially 1 does for multiplication and division what zero does for addition and subtraction. As students discuss the conjectures, it is valuable for them to notice these relations.

TABLE 4.1
Basic Properties of Addition and Multiplication

Number Sentence[1]	Children's Conjectures	T/F, Open Number Sentences
Addition and subtraction involving zero		
1a. $a + 0 = a$	When you add zero to a number, you get the number you started with.	$5{,}467 + 0 = 5{,}467$ $23 + 7 = 23$* $40 + 0 = 400$* $89 + c = 89$
1b. $0 + a = a$	When you add a number to zero, you get that number (you added).	$0 + 5{,}467 = 5{,}467$ $23 + 7 = 7$* $c + 89 = 89$
2. $a - 0 = a$	When you subtract zero from a number, you get the number you started with.	$536 - 0 = 536$ $48 - 9 = 48$* $570 - 0 = 57$* $c - 0 = 654$
3. $a - a = 0$	When you subtract a number from itself, you get zero.	$975 - 975 = 0$ $27 - 35 = 0$* $846 - c = 0$
Multiplication and division involving 1		
4a. $a \times 1 = a$	When you multiply a number times 1, you get the number you started with.	$5{,}467 \times 1 = 5{,}467$ $48 \times 1 = 49$* $8.4 \times .01 = 8.4$* $c \times 1 = 76$
4b. $1 \times a = a$	When you multiply 1 times a number, you get that number.	$1 \times 5{,}467 = 5467$ $1 \times c = 76$
5. $a \div 1 = a$	When you divide a number by 1, you get the number you started with.	$536 \div 1 = 536$ $48 \div 2 = 48$* $c \div 1 = 85$
6. $a \div a = 1, a \neq 0$	When you divide a number by itself, you get 1, except when the number is zero.[2]	$975 \div 975 = 1$ $384 \div 384 = 0$* $2 \div 5 = 0$* $c \div 39 = 1$

TABLE 4.1 continued
*Basic Properties of
Addition and
Multiplication*

Number Sentence[1]	Children's Conjectures	T/F, Open Number Sentences
Multiplication and division involving zero		
7a. $a \times 0 = 0$	When you multiply a number times zero, you get zero.	$345 \times 0 = 0$ $28 \times 0 = 28$* $94 \times c = 0$ $c \times 0 = 0$
7b. $0 \times a = 0$	When you multiply zero times a number, you get zero.	$0 \times 345 = 0$ $0 \times 28 = 28$* $c \times 94 = 0$
8. $0 \div a = 0, a \neq 0$	When you divide zero by any number except zero, you get zero.[3]	$0 \div 35 = 0$ $0 \div 35 = 35$* $c \div 56 = 0$
Commutative properties for addition and multiplication		
9. $a + b = b + a$	When you add two numbers, you can change the order of the numbers you add, and you will still get the same number.	$34 + 58 = 58 + 34$ $95 + 87 = c + 95$
10. $a \times b = b \times a$	When you multiply two numbers, you can change the order of the numbers you multiply, and you will get the same number.	$34 \times 58 = 58 \times 34$ $95 \times 87 = c \times 87$

[1] Note that for an open number sentence to represent a conjecture, it is understood that the number sentence is true for every number that could be substituted for the variable.

[2] Most students do not understand why it is not possible to divide by zero, even those taking algebra in high school. Initially children may not exclude zero in this conjecture. It is not necessarily bad to ignore that when this conjecture is first introduced, but you may want to come back later and edit the conjecture when children address the concept of division by zero. This issue is discussed in some detail in a later chapter.

[3] See footnote 2.

*False number sentence.

Students sometimes extend the conjectures in Table 4.1 by applying one of them multiple times. For example, students might come up with a conjecture such as $a + 0 + 0 + 0 = a$. Although this conjecture is true, it does not add a great deal to the basic conjecture about adding zero, and an infinite number of such conjectures is possible. These issues are interesting to discuss if they come up, and students often show good insight in discussing them.

Students also sometimes write conjectures that are special cases of the conjectures in Table 4.1. The following are valid conjectures: $5 + a = a + 5$, $9 + a = a + 9$, and so on, but it would not be sensible to have all these conjectures when $a + b = b + a$ covers them all. We would like to be economical in writing conjectures, so having one conjecture that does the work of many is something to strive for. If conjectures like these come up, they can provide an opportunity to discuss what makes some conjectures better than others.

It is possible to combine conjectures in useful ways to generate new conjectures. The conjectures in Table 4.2 are a little different from the conjectures in Table 4.1 in that they can be derived from them. Conjecture 11 combines Conjectures 3 and 1, and Conjecture 12 combines Conjectures 6 and 4. They are included here because students often identify these relations among these conjectures, and as a consequence they provide a good context for discussing how students know that a conjecture is true for all numbers. We will talk more about how these conjectures may be derived and justified in Chapter 7, when we discuss justification and proof.

TABLE 4.2
Conjectures Derived from Basic Properties

Number Sentence	Children's Conjectures	T/F, Open Number Sentences
11. $a + b - b = a$	When you add a number to another number and then subtract the number you added, you get the number you started with.	$47 + 78 - 78 = 47$ $56 + 67 - 67 = 67*$ $94 + 79 - c = 94$
12. $a \times b \div b = a$ $b \neq 0$	When you multiply a number by another number that is not zero and then divide by the same number, you get the number you started with.	$47 \times 78 \div 78 = 47$ $96 \times 32 \div 32^* = 32$ $7.9 \times .06 \div d = 7.9$

Invalid Conjectures

In the process of generating and discussing conjectures like those listed in Table 4.1, children sometimes generate conjectures that look a lot like valid conjectures but are not true. Some of the most common cases are listed in Table 4.3.

The incorrect conjectures look very much like extensions of valid conjectures, but in these cases the extensions are based on form rather than on mathematical principles. Students have overgeneralized that because addition and multiplication are commutative, subtraction and division are also.

TABLE 4.3
*Some Incorrect
Conjectures about
Number Operations*

Number Sentence	Statement of the Conjecture	T/F, Open Number Sentences
13. $0 - a = a$	When you subtract a number from zero, you get the number you started with.	$0 - 536 = 536$*
14. $a \div 0 = 0$, $a \div 0 = 1$	When you divide any number by zero, you get zero (or 1).	$25 \div 0 = 0$* $0 \div 0 = 0$* $0/0 = 1$*
15. $a - b = b - a$	When you subtract two numbers, you can change the order of the numbers you subtract, and you will still get the same number.	$94 - 37 = 37 - 94$* $8 - 17 = 9$*
16. $a \div b = b \div a$	When you divide two numbers, you can change the order of the numbers you divide, and you will get the same answer.	$56 \div 8 = 8 \div 56$* $7 \div 42 = 6$*

MORE CONJECTURES

The conjectures listed so far represent basic properties of addition, subtraction, multiplication, and division. These properties are fundamental and, together with a few additional properties that we will discuss later, make possible most of the manipulations we do with numbers and algebraic expressions. Virtually all procedures for adding, subtracting, multiplying, and dividing numbers and for solving equations and simplifying algebraic expressions depend on these properties. We discuss how computational algorithms and algebra depend on these properties in Chapters 7 and 8.

TEACHER COMMENTARY 4.4

My students thought that there were no numbers smaller than zero. When they subtracted a larger number from a smaller number, they got zero. For example, when I asked them to solve $5 - 8$, they said the answer would be zero. I shared this in our algebra workshop and someone suggested that I try an open number sentence like $25 - \square = 0$. So I did. Right away one child said "twenty-five." I asked, "Is that the only number that will make this true?"

Another child said that 30 would also work, but someone disagreed with that. She said, "No, if you have 25 dollars and you spend 30 dollars, you are going to have to borrow some money or something and then you will owe someone money. It is not the same as zero because you still owe money."

We discussed this for awhile and most of the kids agreed that only 25 could go in the box. I asked them if they noticed something that would always be true. Many kids said yes and started talking about taking away the same number that you started with. Someone eventually said, "If you have a number and you subtract the same number, you will get zero." I wrote that down word for word and told the kids it was a conjecture.

Just to see what would happen, I then asked the kids, "Zero is a special number. Do you notice anything else about zero?" Within the next five minutes we had two more conjectures: "When you take zero away from a number, you will get the same number," and "If you have a number and add zero, you will still have the same number you started with." I was really amazed that my kids came up with three conjectures like that. For the rest of the math class, I had them get into groups of three and write number sentences that went with each of the conjectures. All the groups could do it. It was great.

Katie Mahr, First-grade teacher

As children generate conjectures based on true/false and open number sentences, generating conjectures becomes an ongoing process that is not limited by the problems posed by the teacher. Children do not, however, limit themselves to these conjectures, they usually wind up making all sorts of conjectures about numbers and operations on them. Some of the conjectures may be similar to those listed previously; others may deal with other observations that are interesting to the children. For example, consider the following interaction in a beginning second-grade class just starting to generate conjectures.

Robin: I have another one. If you add two numbers, you get a bigger number.

Ms. J.:   [*Writes the conjecture on a sheet of paper*] What do you all think about this? Is it always true?

There is a general nodding of heads. Nobody volunteers that it is not true for all numbers.

Ms. J.:   Is it at all like any of our other conjectures?

Thomas: Wait a minute. Zero. Zero plus any number is that number. So that's not always true.

Robin: I mean any number except zero.

Ms. J.:   So, Robin, are you saying you want to edit your conjecture?

Robin: Yeah. If you add two numbers except zero, you get a bigger number.

Ms. J.:   [*Inserts "except zero" in the conjecture*] How is that now?

*The class affirms that it is okay now. Ms. J. has a decision to make. The chil-
dren are generally happy with the conjecture, but the statement of the conjecture is somewhat ambiguous. None of the children seem inclined to raise the
issue, so she asks a question to further the discussion.*

Ms. J.:   Bigger than what?
Jackie: Bigger than the number you are adding; bigger than
               either number you are adding.
Ms. J.:   Should we make that part of the conjecture?

*The class agrees that they should, and the conjecture is modified to read: When
you add two numbers except zero, you get a number bigger than either of the
numbers you added.*

Now Ms. J. is faced with a more difficult decision. As stated, the conjecture is not correct if negative numbers are taken into account. The children, however, have not talked about negative numbers. Ms. J. has several
options:

1. She could let the conjecture stand as it is. It is true for the numbers
   that the children have studied, and the students are happy with it.
   Ms. J. is troubled, however, by this option. She does not want to
   have the children learn a principle that is not true for all numbers,
   even those they have not learned about yet, so she rejects this
   option.
2. She could edit the conjecture slightly so that it would be true: *When
   you add two numbers larger than zero, you get a number larger than
   either of the numbers you added.* She might just make the change
   without talking about the reason, or she might say that there are
   some numbers that the class has not talked about yet that result in a
   smaller number when added to another number.
3. She could take this as an opportunity to introduce negative numbers, either briefly or more extensively. Depending on how much
   detail she wanted to go into, that could involve a major commitment of time.

There are several interesting issues raised by this interaction. One is the
question of how to deal with a conjecture that is not true for all numbers. It
is particularly problematic in cases in which children have not studied
numbers that would make the statement false. If children do not have any
basis for recognizing the limitations of a conjecture, they are likely to accept
as valid for all numbers a conjecture that is only true for the numbers they
have studied. On the other hand, we would like children to take responsibility for deciding whether conjectures are true or false so that the teacher is
not the final arbiter. Our position is that it probably is a good idea not to
leave children with the impression that a conjecture is true for all numbers
when it actually is true only for a limited set of numbers. This does
not mean that we believe that the teacher should step in immediately when
a false conjecture is proposed—quite the contrary. We definitely want

children to take that responsibility, and it is not necessarily bad if a conjecture is posted that is not true, as long as the truth of the conjecture is recognized as in doubt.

A second issue is that this kind of conjecture is quite different from the basic conjectures about number operations that we considered earlier in this chapter. The set of conjectures listed in Table 4.1 are essential properties of number operations that are critical for understanding and justifying the basic operations of arithmetic. The conjecture about the relative size of the sum of two numbers may have some relevance for eliminating some clearly incorrect answers to calculations, but it is quite different from the conjectures in Table 4.1. It may be worth having some discussion about different kinds of conjectures to see if students can recognize a difference between these types of conjectures and those listed in Table 4.1.

One of the most constructive aspects of discussing this sort of conjecture may be realized through editing initial conjectures. For example, many children implicitly use an incorrect assumption about multiplication to make decisions about whether to multiply or divide. The assumption is: *When two numbers are multiplied, the answer is larger than either of the numbers.* As with the conjecture about adding discussed earlier, the conjecture needs to be qualified. *When two numbers that are larger than 1 are multiplied, the answer is larger than either of the numbers.* Explicitly discussing and editing this conjecture may help students avoid the misconception that multiplication makes bigger and division makes smaller.

Definitions

Children frequently propose conjectures that are definitions. For example, they may suggest the following conjecture: *When an even number is divided by 2, there is nothing left over.* At the primary grades the definition might be stated as: *If you have an even number of counters, you can divide them into two equal groups and there won't be any left over.* Although there are alternative ways that even numbers can be defined, these statements represent definitions of even numbers. Another conjecture that children might propose is: *A prime number is any whole number (greater than 1) that is only divisible by 1 and itself.* Again, this statement represents a definition rather than a conjecture. A critical distinction between definitions and the other conjectures we have been discussing is that there is no way to justify a definition. We define terms so that we know what we are talking about. But definitions are somewhat arbitrary. It is the way it is because it is defined to be that way. In contrast, children can justify why the conjectures in Table 4.1 are valid. For the conjectures in Table 4.1, the question "How do you know that is always true?" is an interesting one. For definitions, the answer is: "Because it is defined that way."

So where does this leave us with regard to conjectures and definitions? The way we are defining conjectures, they are different from definitions, and it is important that children understand the difference. Making this distinction can be very informative. Often students do not recognize the distinction, and they do not clearly distinguish what is a definition and what is not. They may have multiple definitions and not appreciate that it is necessary to be sure that the different definitions are equivalent. Thus, for many of the same reasons that we want students to articulate and be precise about conjectures, we want them to articulate and be precise about definitions. Most students have a difficult time carefully defining mathematical terms that they are familiar with. For example, most high school students know what a triangle is, but few of them can give an accurate definition of a triangle in words. We want students to distinguish between conjectures and definitions, but it is equally appropriate to engage students in articulating and editing definitions.

Rules for Carrying Out Procedures

Students also propose conjectures that are rules for carrying out procedures. A common procedural rule that students often are taught is: *When you multiply a number by 10, you can just add a zero to the right of the number.* There are problems with this statement, some quite serious. First of all, although most students implicitly figure out what to do, what does it mean to add a zero to the right of the number? For example, $75 + 0 = 75$, not 750. Perhaps even more critical, the statement as it stands is not true for decimals ($10 \times 7.46 \neq 7.460$). The corresponding statement for decimals might say something about moving the decimal point one place to the right. But still, it would require some cleaning up to meet our emerging standards of accuracy. Many of us use these rules. They can be convenient. But they have to do with generating answers, not developing understanding of fundamental properties of number operations. Once again, we propose that if you and your students want to include such rules in your list of conjectures, you distinguish them from the conjectures that represent fundamental properties of numbers.

Conjectures About Even and Odd Numbers

If children have been introduced to even and odd numbers, they may generate conjectures about them such as: *When you add two odd numbers, you get an even number.* Although conjectures about even and odd numbers are more limited in scope than the basic conjectures listed in Table 4.1, these conjectures can provide a good site for students to generate and justify conjectures. Some of the conjectures are not entirely obvious to children, so that generating conjectures can involve some exploration. As we will discuss in later chapters, conjectures about even and odd numbers can be justified at a number of different levels. As a consequence, conjectures about even and odd numbers offer a good opportunity to examine what it means to justify a conjecture.

SUMMARY: TYPES OF CONJECTURES THAT STUDENTS MAKE

There are a number of ways we could sort conjectures, but we have found that it is useful to think about them in terms of five basic classes:

- *Conjectures about fundamental properties of number operations* are conjectures like those listed in Table 4.1 that describe basic properties of numbers and operations on them. These conjectures represent important ideas about arithmetic that make the learning of arithmetic easier and that are critical for learning algebra. In the long run, these are the most important conjectures for students' learning of arithmetic and algebra. We will introduce additional conjectures of this type in Chapters 8 and 9.

- *Conjectures about classes of numbers* include conjectures about even and odd numbers. They also include conjectures about factors and divisibility rules (e.g., *A whole number is divisible by 5 if it ends in 0 or 5*).

- *Descriptions of procedures* are rules for carrying out specific computational procedures. Common examples include rules for multiplying by 10 or 100. These are quite different from conjectures about fundamental properties of number operations. One important difference between the two types of conjectures is that conjectures about fundamental properties involve relations that generally can be expressed simply as open number sentences that are always true (e.g., $a + b = b + a$), whereas descriptions of procedures involve outcomes of calculations that usually are not amenable to being expressed in terms of open number sentences.

- *General descriptions of outcomes of calculations* include such notions as addition and multiplication resulting in larger numbers, given the appropriate conditions on the numbers involved in the calculations. The conjectures of this kind that most young children come up with often are quite global conjectures regarding the magnitude of the results of calculations, but conjectures about the magnitudes of calculations can be more specific as well. Following is an example of a more specific and consequently more useful conjecture: *If a is greater than b and c is greater than d, then a + c is greater than b + d.*

- *Definitions.* Definitions probably should not be considered as conjectures at all, but they do come up as students are generating conjectures about number properties, and they need to be distinguished from these conjectures. Whereas justifying conjectures is an important issue that we will get to in subsequent chapters, definitions cannot be justified. They are true by definition.

Although students might not come up with exactly these distinctions among conjectures, they can recognize important differences, and if a variety of conjectures such as those listed previously is generated, it can be worthwhile to engage students in a discussion of differences among the conjectures they have generated.

TEACHER COMMENTARY 4.5

Mathematics instruction in my class is heavily dependent on language. Children use their receptive language as they listen to each other's ideas and to the problems I pose; they make use of expressive language as they share their ideas and ask questions. Eventually they even write their ideas, sometimes in the form of conjectures. This can be challenging for special education kids or other kids who have language difficulties. Still, it is so critical to have all kids participate in this type of mathematics instruction. Kids who have language difficulties need to be immersed in language. If language is a part of mathematics, it has to be good for their development, both in language and in mathematics. If these kids were to get something more traditional, something where language was less crucial to their success, it might appear that they were succeeding. For example, many kids can learn to do workbook pages very well. But when it comes time to use these concepts in a practical setting or in solving a problem, they won't be able to do it. Also, their engagement in these traditional activities would do nothing to advance their language skills. When children can actually write something like, "If you have a number and you add zero to that number, you get the number you started with," it really tells me something about their mathematical and language development. They feel comfortable expressing their thinking with words and are expressing a complex idea in an accurate and concise manner. Oftentimes they don't get it right the first time and have to go back, add information, and change some words to clarify their thinking. For first and second graders, the fact that they can do this is just amazing.

Virginia Koberstein, First- and second-grade teacher

CHALLENGES

1. Construct a series of true/false and open number sentences that might be used to elicit each of the conjectures in Table 4.1.
2. For at least two of the conjectures, try the number sentences you constructed with your class or a small group of students. How did they respond?
3. What conjectures about even and odd numbers do you think your students might be able to come up with? Share your conjectures and discuss how they may be edited to make them more accurate or understandable.

5 | EQUATIONS WITH MULTIPLE VARIABLES AND REPEATED VARIABLES

In Chapters 2 and 3 we looked at open number sentences with a single unknown. For those number sentences, students were asked to find the number that could be substituted for the unknown to make the number sentence true. In this chapter we expand the discussion to include number sentences such as $x + y = 7$. In this case, x and y are variables, and there are many numbers that can be substituted for x and y to make this number sentence true. We extend the range of number sentences further by introducing equations in which a variable is repeated and consider the kinds of mathematical thinking that these kinds of number sentences afford.

We start with a problem situation that provides a context for thinking about number sentences involving several variables. Next we consider some different equations with multiple variables and repeated variables and the mathematical ideas that may emerge as children solve them.

As in the preceding chapters, our goal is not simply to introduce children to algebraic notation and procedures but rather to provide a basis for using algebraic notation and algebraic reasoning to enrich the study of arithmetic by focusing on important mathematical ideas and ways of thinking.

CAGED MICE: A CONTEXT FOR INTRODUCING MULTIPLE VARIABLES

Consider the following problem:

> *Ricardo has 7 pet mice. He keeps them in two cages that are connected so that the mice can go back and forth between the cages. One of the cages is big and the other is small. Show all the ways that 7 mice can be in two cages.*[1]

The mathematical goal of this problem is to list all the ways that seven things can be partitioned into two groups. The problem is open to a wide range of solutions representing different levels of understanding of the situation. At the most basic level, students list combinations as they occur to them. At more advanced levels, students recognize that part of the problem is to find a way to organize their answer to show that they have included all possible combinations. One of the first issues encountered by students in solving this problem is finding a good way to record their answers. Some teachers have used the problem as a context for engaging students in a discussion of notation. These teachers have first allowed students to record answers in any way they chose, and then made the utility and clarity of different ways of recording answers a specific focus of discussion. In the following class episode, the second-grade teacher introduces the notation to record answers as she presents the problem.

Ms. S.: [*Reads the problem and then asks*] Who can tell us one way that the mice might be in the two cages?

Robin: There could be 5 in the big cage and 2 in the little cage.

Ms. S.: Raise your hand if you agree that is one possibility. [*All the students raise their hands.*] Okay. Let's write that down. [*Ms. S. makes two columns and writes "Big Cage" above one column and "Small Cage" above the other. She writes 5 in the Big Cage column and 2 in the Small Cage column.*] Can anyone think of another possibility?

Erica: Four and 3.

Ms. S.: Where are the 4 mice?

Erica: In the big cage.

Ms. S.: So where should I write that?

Jan: Under the 5, and put 3 under the 2.

Ms. S.: [*Writes 4 and 3 in the appropriate columns*] Now I want you each to write as many different ways as you can that the mice might be in the two cages.

As the students start to work, Ms. S. circulates among them. She notices that there is no pattern to most students' answers. A number of students do not have a pair with all the mice in one of the cages, and several students do not include combinations that reverse the number of mice in the two cages [e.g., (3,4) and (4,3)] After most of the students appear to have written all

---

[1]Often this problem needs some clarification. We have found the easiest way to clarify the problem is to do one or two cases as a group so students understand what is expected. One of the alternative interpretations that students sometimes have for this problem is that the combinations are different depending on which mice are in a given cage. For example, there would be 21 different combinations with 2 mice in the big cage and 5 mice in the small cage. Mickey Mouse and Minnie Mouse in the bigger cage would count as a different combination than Mickey Mouse and Mighty Mouse. That is an interesting but much more difficult problem. There are 128 different combinations of that kind for 7 mice.

the possibilities that they can think of, Ms. S. gathers the class together to share their answers. She could ask different students to contribute different combinations, but since she wants students to think about different ways that students have generated their answers, she asks several students to come to the front of the group and show the list of combinations they have generated. The first two students share the following lists:

	Big Cage	Small Cage			Big Cage	Small Cage
Steve's list	5	2		Aaron's list	5	2
	4	3			4	3
	6	1			2	5
					1	6
					3	4
					6	1

There is a discussion of the two lists. At first Steve and several other students object that Aaron has put the same thing down twice, but the class resolves that 5 mice in the big cage and 2 in the small cage is different from 2 in the big cage and 5 in the small cage. Everyone sees that this gives them more possibilities. Ms. S. calls on two more students to share.

	Big Cage	Small Cage			Big Cage	Small Cage
Rico's list	5	2		Sandra's list	5	2
	4	3			2	5
	1	6			4	3
	0	7			3	4
	7	0			6	1
	2	5			1	6
	6	1				

Rico added the possibility of having all the mice in one cage and none in the other, and Sandra's list has an interesting pattern. As they compare the lists, the students recognize that Rico's list is the longest, but when (7,0) and (0,7) are added to Sandra's and Aaron's lists they are longer than Rico's. One student recognizes that Rico left out (3,4).

Ms. S.: Sandra, there is an interesting pattern in the way you wrote the numbers in your list. Do you want to tell us about that?

Sandra: Well I knew that when I had it one way, like 5 mice in the big cage and 2 in the little cage, I could just turn it around. So it would be 2 and 5. And it's like that with all the numbers.

Ms. S.: Did anyone get a pair that is not up here? [*No students respond that they have a different pair.*] Do you think we have all the possibilities in the lists we have on the board? [*The students are not sure, but after looking at the lists, most of them seem to think that they have all the possibilities.*] How can we be sure that we have all the possibilities? Some of you thought you had them all, but you missed some.

The students cannot resolve the problem right away, but they return to it the next day. The four lists from the preceding day are still posted on the board.

Ms. S.: Let's think about the question we asked yesterday: How can we be sure that we have all the possibilities? Look at the lists we have here; can any of them help you decide?

Rico: Sandra's list. If we had one more, we would have two more. I don't think there are two more.

Ms. S.: Does that help us be sure there aren't any more?

Rico: No. But it doesn't seem like there could be two more.

Jenny: I have an idea. If you look at Sandra's list, she has a cage with 5 in it, and then a cage with 2 in it, and then 4 and 3. And 6 and 1, and 7 and 0. She has used all the numbers.

Ms. S.: I don't quite get what you are saying. Can you show us on Sandra's list?

Jenny: See, here's 5, and 2, and 4, and 3, and 6, and 1, and 7, and 0. That's all the ways it could be, cause that's all the numbers there are. [*As she says the numbers, she points to the numbers in the first column.*]

Ms. S.: Oh, I see. Jenny, you are saying that you can put 5 mice in the big cage, or 2, or any of these numbers [*gesturing to the first column*], and those are the only possibilities with 7 mice. Is there a way we could write that to make it easier to see? [*Many of the students are still not seeing what Jenny is talking about, but Marsha excitedly raises her hand.*]

Marsha: You could go 1, 2, 3, 4, 5, 6, 7, and 0.

Ms. S.: Maybe you should write it down, Marsha.

Marsha writes 1, 2, 3, 4, 5, 6, 7, 0 in a column. When she is done, she writes 6, 5, 4, 3, 2, 1, 0, 7 next to the appropriate numbers, as shown in the following table:

	Big Cage	Small Cage
	1	6
	2	5
	3	4
Marsha's	4	3
list	5	2
	6	1
	7	0
	0	7

The students discuss this table and why it helps them show that they have found all the possibilities. They go on to solve several similar problems. By the end of the week, some of the students make the conjecture that the number of possibilities is always one more than the number of mice. When asked how many possibilities there are for 52 mice or 147 mice, they can respond without listing all the possibilities. Later in the year the class returns to this problem. The students remember the problem, easily generate the possibilities, and predict how many possibilities there would be for any given number of mice.

Ms. S.: How about 324 mice?

Jamie: It would be 325.

Anna: Yeah, it's always just one more than the number of mice. These are easy.

Ms. S.: Oh, how about if there are *n* mice?

Anna: It would be just one more than that.

Ms. S.: How would we write that? [*The children struggle with this question for a while. Finally Carla responds.*]

Carla: Would it be $n + 1$?

Several features of this entire episode are significant in terms of students' mathematical engagement. At first most children generate combinations without much order or thought of mathematical properties. Sandra's solution shows more insight, as she applies the commutative property of addition. Next the children grapple with the problem of justifying that they have all the solutions. This leads them to a conjecture about the number of solutions for any number of mice. Finally they express this conjecture using algebraic notation. We talked about conjectures in the previous chapter. In the following chapters, we discuss justifying conjectures and expressing them using algebraic notation. This activity provides a context for beginning to engage students with these ideas.

TEACHER COMMENTARY 5.1

I like to give problems like the mice-and-two-cages problem to my students. However, with this type of problem there is likely to be more explanation than typical. No matter how well you write these problems, you will always need to make the parameters clear for some students. You might get a kid who says a mouse can be half in one cage and half in the other. Another kid might say, "What if we have three brown mice in the little cage and one brown mouse and three white mice in the big cage and a different way could be three white mice in the little cage and four brown mice in the big cage?" Kids like to think outside the box and I like to encourage that, but you miss the whole point of the problem if you allow these types of solutions.

Once the kids understand the problem, the next confusion comes in keeping track of the solutions. Some kids might make pictures or write out the words to help them, but other kids will have no organization scheme at all. As kids start sharing solutions, it quickly becomes evident that we need some way of keeping track of what has been said. I usually record their solutions on a T-chart. I label one column *Big Cage*, the other column *Small Cage*. Most kids quickly see what I am doing. The T-chart helps in their reflection; they can see if they have the commutative pairs. If there is a 1 and a 6 up there, there also has to be a 6 and a 1. It is also a way of understanding that these pairs are different. The T-chart also helps them to see if they have all the different pairs. Some kids learn that they can just look in one column and make sure they have all the counting numbers from 0 to the number of mice or whatever.

I like to do problems like this throughout the year. I really know they understand when they can just go to a problem and say, "Hey, this is just like the one we did with the mice." Sometimes I will pose something like $a + b = 7$ and some kids will say, "This is just like the mice problem." They do soon see that there are more solutions like fractions and negative numbers, but really the concept is the same. When kids make this connection, I know they really understand.

Sue Berthouex, Second- and third-grade teacher

A RELATED PROBLEM WITH NUMBER SENTENCES

The problem we have just discussed can be represented using number sentences. One number sentence for the problem Ms. S. posed to her students would be $w + y = 7$. The question is: What numbers can we put in for w and y to make this a true number sentence? To make the problem similar to the one solved by Ms. S.' students, we would have to limit the domain of possible answers to whole numbers. The context of Ms. S.' problem limited the possibilities to whole numbers (unless a farmer's wife with a carving knife were involved), but the equation $w + y = 7$ allows answers other than whole numbers [e.g., $(5\frac{1}{2}, 1\frac{1}{2})$, $(\frac{3}{4}, 6\frac{1}{4})$, $(2.456, 4.544)$] unless specified otherwise. On the other hand, children in first or second grade who have limited exposure to fractions and fraction addition can deal productively with equations like $w + y = 7$ even though the solutions they generate are likely to be limited to whole numbers.

Number sentences like $w + y = 7$ are somewhat different from the open number sentences that we discussed in the previous chapters in which students found a value for an unknown that would make the number sentence true. In number sentences like $w + y = 7$, w and y are *variables*; there are many numbers that can be substituted for w and y to make this number sentence true. These number sentences open up a number of options for students to engage in mathematical thinking and to use algebraic notation to express mathematical ideas. As in the preceding chapters, our goal is not simply to introduce children to algebraic notation and procedures; rather, it is to provide a basis for using algebraic notation and algebraic reasoning to enrich the study of arithmetic by focusing on important mathematical ideas and ways of thinking.

These number sentences can be introduced without a great deal of fanfare, just as number sentences with a single unknown are introduced. In the following episode, students have been solving open number sentences with a single unknown when Ms. W. gives the following problem:

Ms. W.: What can we put in for s and t so that this number sentence is true: $s + t = 8$? [*After some initial confusion, the students begin to respond.*]

Jason: Three and 5 will work. If I put in 3 for s, and 5 for t, it's 8.

Sarah: But I got 6 and 2. They work, too.

Ms. W.: Can both of those answers be right?

Sarah: Yeah. They both work.

Ms. W.: Did anybody find a different one?

The class continues to generate combinations for s and t. One student recognizes that this is the same thing that they did with the mice in cages, and they decide that they can use the same kinds of tables to write down their answers. The students recognize that there are many numbers that they can pick for s, but once they pick a number for s, there is only one number that they can replace t with to make the sentence true. Alternatively, they can start by choosing a number for t, and then find the replacement for s that will make the sentence true.

Other number sentences result in different patterns of answers and different generalizations. For example, for the number sentence $p - r = 6$, students might observe that there is no limit to the number of pairs of numbers that can be substituted for p and r, even when the domain of possible answers is limited to whole numbers. They might observe that p is always 6 more than r and that if the possibilities are limited to whole numbers, then p must be 6 or larger. For the number sentence $2 \times v + y = 14$, students might observe that v can be either even or odd, but when v is a whole number, y has to be an even number.

NUMBER SENTENCES WITH VARIABLES
APPEARING MORE THAN ONCE

In the last section, we saw that number sentences with several variables had many solutions. How about number sentences like $w + w = 12$? To decide what number or numbers we can replace w with to make this a true sentence, we need to know whether there are restrictions on the numbers we can substitute. There are a couple of options. Can we put one number in for the first w and a different number for the second w, or do we have to put the same number in for both? The second option is the one that mathematicians have agreed to adopt.

> When the same variable appears more than one time in a number sentence, the variable must be replaced by the same number throughout the number sentence for each substitution.

For example, 6 is the only number that can be substituted in the number sentence $w + w = 12$ to make the number sentence true. For the number sentence $c + c + c = 12$, 4 is the only substitution for c that will make the sentence true. For $5 \times r - r = 20$, $r = 5$, and for $g + g = 9$, $g = 4\,^1/_2$.

This convention, which many of the classes we have worked with call *the mathematicians' rule,* can be introduced when discussing a specific number sentence that requires it, as illustrated in the following scenario.

Ms. J.:   What can we put in for s to make this a true number sentence: $s + s = 10$?

Simon: This is like the ones we did yesterday. There are a lot of things we could put in. We could put in 1 for the first s and 9 for the second. We could put in 2 and 8, 3 and 7. . . .

Ms. J.:   [*Interrupting*] Okay, before you go on, does anybody see anything different about this number sentence and the ones we did yesterday?

Grace: This one has an s added to another s. Yesterday the letters were different.

Ms. J.:   That turns out to be an important difference. There is a rule that I haven't told you about yet that applies to this problem. When we have the same letter or symbol in a number sentence, we have to put in the same number for each one. We can't put one number in for the first one and a different number in for the second. So what is the solution for this one [$s + s = 10$]?

Randy: Five.

Ms. J.:   Are there any other numbers that would work?

Gloria: No.

The class continues looking at different examples of number sentences in which the same variable appears more than once.

Solving Equations

Once students have learned the rule for dealing with number sentences with repeated variables, they can attempt to solve number sentences that challenge their mathematical thinking. The primary goal in giving students these number sentences is not to teach students efficient ways to solve algebra equations; it is to engage them in thinking flexibly about number operations and relations. These problems provide an opportunity to extend the kind of relational thinking discussed in Chapter 3. By comparing alternative strategies, students are challenged to think about number operations in different ways. They may start to see the operations on numbers as more than just procedures to be carried out in a step-by-step sequence. They may start to appreciate the power that understanding the properties of these operations brings them. Following are some examples of students' solutions of different number sentences.

Number sentence: $d + d - 5 = 13$

Susan: First I tried 6, and that was too small: 6 plus 6 is 12 and 12 minus 5 is 7. So I tried a bigger number, 10. Ten and 10 is 20, take away 5 is 15, so that's too big. So I tried 9, and 9 plus 9 is 18 and take away 5 is 13. So it's 9.

Erika: I knew 18 minus 5 is 13. So d plus d had to be 18, and that meant d had to be 9, cause 9 plus 9 equals 18.

Susan uses trial and error. She substitutes numbers starting at the left and carries out the calculations from left to right. She appears to understand how to deal with the repeated unknown. Her strategy is valid, and her answer is correct. But her solution shows less insight than Erika's does. Erika is more flexible in her thinking. She thinks about the expression on the left of the equal sign as an entity that is equal to 13, and she is able to unpack that expression. The only number given in the expression is 5, so she starts there. She sees that 5 is subtracted from $d + d$ to give 13. She knows that $18 - 5$ is 13, so she reasons that $d + d$ must be 18. This is quite sophisticated. It requires thinking of $d + d$ as a number. That is not straightforward for many children. Once Erika reasons that $d + d = 18$, the rest is relatively straightforward.

Number sentence: $3 \times p + p + 2 - p = 17$

Susan: First I tried 4. Three times 4 is 12, and 4 more is 16 and 2 is 18, take away 4; that's 14. Too small, so I tried a bigger number, 6. That was too big, so I tried 5, and that came out right. Three times 5 is 15, and 5 more is 20, and 2 is 22, take away 5 is 17.

Erika: Well, there is a *p* and you take away a *p*, so it's like it was never there. So it's like 3 times *p* plus 2 equals 17, and 15 and 2 is 17. So 3 times *p* is 15, and that makes *p* 5.

Once again Susan uses trial and error. There are more calculations, but the process is basically similar to the process she used on the preceding problem. Erika considers the problem as a whole before she starts to calculate. She recognizes that *p* is added and subtracted, so these two *p*s cancel each other out. This simplifies the problem considerably, and she is able to proceed much as she did in the preceding problem.

Number sentence: $6 \times q = 2 \times q + 24$

Erika: Well I have these 2 *q*s over here and 6 over here, and the 6 times *q* is the same as 2 times *q* plus 24. So that means that 4 times *q* equals 24, because the 6 times *q* is like 2 times *q* plus 4 times *q*. The 2 times *q* on each side are the same, so the 4 times *q* and the 24 have to be the same. So it's 6, because 4 times 6 equals 24.

We want to reiterate that the solutions we have described are solutions that students have figured out for themselves. The reason for having students solve equations like these is to provide students opportunity to explore relationships involving operations on numbers. It is not to teach students algebra procedures or efficient methods for solving equations. Rather, students have an opportunity to extend their ability to use relational thinking. In later grades, students will learn more efficient procedures for solving equations. The value in solving these equations using these more informal methods is in the process. Even the students using trial and error can be engaged in worthwhile mathematical tasks as they attempt to estimate what numbers they should select to try and how to select the next number based on the results of the calculations for earlier trials.

TEACHER COMMENTARY 5.2

I got good grades in high school algebra. I learned the procedures that the teacher demonstrated. I thought that was what mathematics was about; if you could memorize a procedure then you could do math. I didn't even know that I didn't understand math because I didn't know that understanding was part of math. A couple of years ago, I watched Kevin, a student who struggled with math, solve the problem $2 + d + d = 12$. He took out 12 cubes, took 2 away from the pile of 12 and then split up the remaining cubes into two equal piles. No one taught Kevin this strategy. Kevin's method made me think of the algebraic procedures I was taught. First subtract the 2 from both sides, and then divide the remaining number by 2 to get your answer. When I was in high school, I did not understand the reasons for this procedure; I was only memorizing the steps my teacher taught me. By watching Kevin solve this problem in a way that was meaningful to him, I learned why those steps make sense. As I engage with kids as they solve algebra problems, my understanding of algebra grows. The variety of strategies that the students use to solve these types of problems is fascinating to me. I have become a confident problem solver by working to understand my kids' strategies. Now I want to learn more math because I know I can learn more and I will learn it with understanding.

Kathy Statz, Third-grade teacher

Number Sentences with Several Variables

The mathematicians' rule also applies to number sentences with several variables. A number sentence like $v + v + y = 14$ has many solutions, but in each substitution the same number has to be substituted for each v. For example, if 4 is substituted for v, then $4 + 4 = 8$, so y must be 6. But 1 can also be substituted for v, and in that case, y would be 12. The whole number solutions for $v + v + y = 14$ are listed here:

v	y
0	14
1	12
2	10
3	8
4	6
5	4
6	2
7	0

A Different Use of Notation

Textbooks and other curriculum materials often include problems like the following:

Find the different numbers you can put in the boxes: $\square + \square = 9$.

We believe this is an unfortunate use of notation. The authors are not using the $\square$ as a variable. But this notation can be confusing and contribute to developing misconceptions about how variables are used. It would be preferable to use a number sentence such as $\square + \Delta = 9$. Nevertheless, students may encounter problems in which symbols are not used as variables and do not follow the rules that we have described in this chapter. If this happens, probably the best recourse is to explain that the text is not using the symbol as a variable in the way it is used in algebra.

A Common Misconception

When students learn that the same variable must be replaced by the same number, they often overgeneralize to assume that when the variables are different, they cannot be replaced by the same number. For example, they assume that 4 cannot be substituted for both w and z in the number sentence $w + z = 8$. They often are quite adamant in their assertion that you cannot put in the same number for different variables, and it often takes quite a lot to get them to abandon this conception. This is another interesting subject for class discussion, but once again it is by convention that we allow the same number to be substituted for different variables.

Convenient Conventions

The rule for substituting numbers in an equation in which a variable appears more than once is a convention that people who use mathematics agree to accept, but like the use of the equal sign, the convention makes sense and is useful. When we add three numbers like $4 + 4 + 4$, it is the same as multiplying 3×4. Following the same reasoning, we would expect $c + c + c$ to be the same as $3 \times c$, and therefore we would expect $c + c + c = 12$ to have the same solution as $3 \times c = 12$. Furthermore, we already have a way to write number sentences that allow different substitutions; just use different variables.

By the same token, the fact that the same number can be substituted for different variables is also a convention that is not entirely arbitrary. One important reason to allow the same number for different variables is to provide a match between number sentences and problem situations that they may represent. Consider, for example, a problem similar to the problem at the beginning of this chapter, but with eight mice and two cages. It certainly is possible for four mice to be in each cage, and by the same token, we would want the same possibility to exist for $w + z = 8$.

CHALLENGES

1. Create a problem situation similar to the mouse-cage problem that would be appropriate for your class.
2. Can you create a problem situation similar to the mouse-cage problem that would naturally allow fractions as answers?
3. Write some number sentences involving two variables that would be appropriate for your class. Describe how students might solve them.

4. Give the number sentences you wrote to your class, and then describe how students solved them. Did they solve them in ways that you expected?

5. Describe different ways that students might solve the following number sentences:

   a. $2 \times s + 5 \times s = 15 + 13$
   b. $16 = 4 - t + 3 \times t$
   c. $15 + p = 2 \times p - 3$
   d. $6 \times w + 43 = 10 + 9 \times w$
   e. $3 \times h = 20 - h$
   f. $25 + 3 \times k = 5 \times k - 7$

6. How do you think students might respond to the following number sentence? $p + 4 = p + 7$

7. Write some number sentences involving repeated variables that might be appropriate for your students. Pick several different students in your class, and describe how you think they would solve them.

8. Give the number sentences you wrote to your class, and describe how students solved them. Did they solve them in ways that you expected?

9. In this chapter, we considered number sentences that had many different solutions and some that had no solutions. The next challenge is to try to write a number sentence that is true no matter what number is substituted for the variable or variables. Can you think of some open number sentences that are true for every number that may be substituted for the variable?

6 | REPRESENTING CONJECTURES SYMBOLICALLY

In Chapter 4, we discussed how children make explicit their conjectures about basic number ideas. As described in that chapter, students initially use words to state their conjectures. But it often is difficult to state conjectures precisely in words, and mathematicians often use symbols to represent mathematical ideas precisely. In Table 4.1, we included a representation of each conjecture using symbols. These representations are often easier to read and write when students have learned the necessary conventions. Once students have been introduced to number sentences with multiple variables and equations in which variables appear more than once, they have the necessary tools to represent conjectures using symbols. In this chapter, we describe two examples in which students began to use symbols to represent conjectures.

REPLACING WORDS WITH SYMBOLS

One of the ways that students may be introduced to writing number sentences to represent conjectures is to pick a specific conjecture and ask whether anyone can think of an open number sentence that says the same thing as a written conjecture. The zero property for addition is a good place to start. Students may require a little support to get started, but once they see one number sentence (e.g., $a + 0 = a$), they can build on that to generate number sentences for other conjectures. Note that for an open number sentence to represent a conjecture, there is an implicit statement that the number sentence is true for every number that could be substituted for the variable.

OPEN NUMBER SENTENCES THAT ARE ALWAYS TRUE

A second possibility is to challenge students to write an open number sentence that is true for all numbers. This is a little more challenging than starting with a specific conjecture, but it can result in an interesting discussion.

In the following example, the students struggle at first to figure out what the task is.

Mr. C.: We have been working with number sentences that have had one number we could put in, number sentences that had many different numbers we could put in, and number sentences that didn't have any numbers. Can anyone think of an open number sentence that is always true no matter what number we put in?

Sally: Like 5 plus 6 equals 11. That's always true.

Mr. C.: That is true. Is it an open number sentence?

Class: No.

John: How about q plus r equals s. That can always be true.

Mr. C.: How do you figure that, John?

John: If I put 8 in for q and 5 in for r, then I can put 13 in for s and it will be true. And I can always do that. No matter what I put in for q and r, there will be a number I can put in for s so it will be true.

Mr. C.: Does anybody have any comments about what John has proposed?

Celia: I don't think it is true for all numbers. If you put 8 in for q, and 5 for r, and 10 for s, it would not be true.

John: It would be true if s were 13.

Celia: Yeah, but it is not true for all numbers.

After some discussion, Mr. C. attempts to clarify the problem.

Mr. C.: Let me say the problem again: Can you think of an open number sentence that is always true no matter what number you put in for each of the variables?

The class struggles with the problem for a while longer, until Mr. C. provides a hint to get them started.

Mr. C.: Can you think of any special numbers that you might use?

Rico: *[After a brief pause]* Hey, I have one. How about t plus zero equals t. That's always true no matter what t is.

Mr. C.: What do you think?

The class concurs that it is always true.

Sally: I have another one: a minus zero equals a.

Bret: How about r plus zero plus zero equals r?

Mr. C.: What do you think of that one?

Celia: It's really just kinda like Rico's isn't it? It's still just adding zero. You could do that with any number of zeros; it would never stop.

The class generates additional number sentences involving zero, and also some with 1. Here are the ones they decide are the most important.

$a - a = 0$
$0 \times r = 0$
$1 \times a = a$
$a \div 1 = a$

Several days later, Mr. C. asks the students whether they see any relation between the number sentences they have generated and the conjectures that they have posted around the room. The students realize almost immediately that the number sentences correspond to conjectures they have generated, and they write the number sentences on the papers describing the conjectures. In the process, they come across some conjectures that they do not have number sentences for. They have generated number sentences only for conjectures involving zero and 1, and they do not, for example, have a number sentence that represents the commutative principle for addition. After a bit of struggle, they come up with $a + b = b + a$ and write it on the paper with the commutative property for addition.

TAKING ADVANTAGE OF AN OPPORTUNITY

Sometimes situations arise that provide a natural forum for introducing symbols to represent conjectures. The following interaction took place in a second-grade class. The class was discussing whether or not *Zero plus a number equals that number* and *A number plus zero equals that number* were different conjectures.

Laura: They are different. The first one is like "zero plus number equals number." [*She writes $0 + \# = \#$ on the chalkboard.*] And the other is like "number plus zero equals number." [*She writes $\# + 0 = \#$.*]

Ms. K.: Can anyone else write those conjectures with something other than a number sign?

Mitch wrote $* + 0 = *$ and $0 + * = *$. Carla wrote $\square + 0 = \square$ and $0 + \square = \square$. Jack wrote $m + 0 = m$ and $0 + m = m$.

Ms. K.: Jack just wrote zero plus m equals m. What were you using the m to mean?

Jack: I meant it to mean any number.

Ms. K.: Then we could put any number in there? What if I put a 2 here and an 8 here?

Laura: No you could put a 2 here and a 2 here; you have to put the same thing in both places.

Following this discussion, the students revisited the conjectures they had posted around the room and wrote open number sentences for conjectures that they could represent appropriately that way.

ADVANTAGES OF OPEN NUMBER SENTENCES FOR REPRESENTING CONJECTURES

Open number sentences provide a precise statement of a given conjecture, and students generally agree that it is easier to write many conjectures using open number sentences than it is with words. Open number sentences also make it possible to generate conjectures that are difficult to state in words. For example, the distributive property, $a \times (b + c) = a \times b + a \times c$ is very difficult to express in words, and even a conjecture like $c + b - b = c$ is easier to describe using an open number sentence than in words.

Students also find that some conjectures are not readily expressed using open number sentences. For example, consider the following conjecture: *If you add two numbers larger than zero, the answer is larger than either of the numbers.* There is no simple way to represent this conjecture as an open number sentence. This provides a context for a discussion of differences among conjectures. In general, the conjectures that represent fundamental properties of addition, subtraction, multiplication, and division can be represented with open number sentences.

Finally, using open number sentences provides students with an opportunity to use variables to express mathematical ideas. That is an important mathematical skill, and recognizing that variables can be used for this purpose is an important principle for students to learn. It is a principle that many high school and college students do not fully grasp. For many eighth- and ninth-grade algebra students, algebra involves solving equations for unknowns. For these students, x is an unknown that has a particular value. The idea that letters can represent variables that can be used to represent mathematical relations and express mathematical ideas is foreign to them. These students might view the number sentence $x - x = 0$ as a task to figure out what x equals rather than a way of expressing the general principle that any number minus itself equals zero. This is an extremely limiting perspective that causes problems as students move into more advanced applications of algebra. The multiple perspectives of variables that students are getting in the classes we portray provide a more solid foundation for building algebra concepts and skills.

CHALLENGES

1. Using open number sentences, write as many conjectures as you can that represent important mathematical ideas.
2. Introducing variables to represent conjectures opens the door for students to generate a number of different variations on the conjectures they have written. How would you respond to a student who suggested the following open number sentence as a new conjecture? $b + 0 + 0 - 0 = b$.
3. Can you think of another way that you might introduce open number sentences as a way to represent conjectures?
4. Can you represent an even number using a variable? How about an odd number?

7 | JUSTIFICATION AND PROOF

In Chapter 4, we discussed students' conjectures about mathematical properties of numbers and number operations. In the examples in Chapter 4, children offered some justification for their conjectures, but we did not push very hard on what it would mean to justify that a conjecture was true for all numbers. In this chapter we examine in more depth what it means to justify a conjecture in mathematics.

An important part of learning mathematics is learning what counts as legitimate justification. Mathematicians have established quite rigorous standards of what counts as proof in mathematics. We have chosen to use the term *justification* to encompass a broader range of arguments that children use to show that a conjecture is true. Historically, proof has been the hallmark of the high school geometry course. But justification comes in many forms before students encounter formal proof in high school.

Justification is central to mathematics, and even young children cannot learn mathematics with understanding without engaging in justification. In order to make sense of the concepts and procedures that they are learning, children justify the concepts and procedures to themselves. As they share their ideas and are asked to convince others that a procedure they have used to solve a problem is valid, they have to use arguments that are convincing to other people.

For example, in Chapter 5, we saw students engaged in figuring out how to justify that they had found all the possible combinations of mice in two cages. By explicitly discussing how they could show that they had found all the combinations, the students came up with a way of systematically organizing their combinations that made it clear that they had generated all the possible combinations.

In Chapter 3, we considered how students might use knowledge about number relations to simplify calculations. The arguments they made were essentially justifications for how they knew their answers were correct. For example, consider how one student used relational thinking to simplify the calculations to find the number that makes this a true number sentence: $56 + 47 = 54 + d$.

Ali: Fifty-six is two more than 54, so we take the 2 and put it with the 47. That makes 49, so *d* has to be 49.

Although Ali did not use this notation, his solution could be represented as:

$56 + 47 = (54 + 2) + 47 = 54 + (2 + 47) = 54 + 49.$

In this example, Ali implicitly used knowledge about grouping numbers in addition in order to justify how he figured out the answer.

Another example of this kind of thinking comes up as students justify their thinking as they are learning number facts. For example, Kelly figured out that $6 \times 7 = 42$ by relating it to a number fact that she already knew.

Kelly: I know that 5 times 7 is 35 and 6 times 7 is just 5 times 7 and 7 more $[6 \times 7 = 5 \times 7 + 7]$. So it's 35 and 7. That's 42.

In this example Kelly implicitly used her knowledge of the relation between multiplication and addition to justify how she knew that $6 \times 7 = 42$.

Letting students derive and explain procedures for carrying out multi-digit calculations can provide another opportunity for students to engage in justification implicitly using knowledge of fundamental number properties. For example, consider how Marta explained her solution to 56 + 39:

Marta: Well, 5 and 3 is 8.

Ms. G.:   [*Interrupting*] Where is the 5 and 3?

Marta: Okay, it's 50 and 30. That's like 5 tens and 3 tens. So it's 8 tens; that's 80. And 80 and 6 is 86, and 4 more is 90, and 5 more onto that is 95.

To carry out this calculation, Marta broke the numbers apart and regrouped and reordered the parts in much the same way that Ali did when he used relational thinking.

In all three of these examples, the children implicitly used fundamental properties of number operations as a basis for explaining their procedures. Although none of the three children made explicit the properties that he or she used to regroup and reorder numbers for computation, the children's explanations for why the procedures worked represent a form of justification. In each case, the student derived and explained his or her procedure based on strategies for regrouping and reordering numbers that he or she assumed were valid and would be accepted by the class. Our goal is to build on the kind of reasoning that we see represented in these examples to address more explicitly what is involved in justification in mathematics.

In the previous examples, children implicitly used basic properties of number operations to justify procedures. We have found that elementary school students also can engage productively in justifying that conjectures about basic number properties are true. In fact, as they begin to talk about their conjectures, they recognize the need for better ways of showing that a conjecture is true for all numbers; they see that it is not sufficient simply to give examples that illustrate the conjecture for a few cases or even many cases. In this chapter we consider how students justify conjectures.

LEVELS OF JUSTIFICATION

Students' attempts to justify that mathematical statements are true can be separated into three broad classes:

- appeal to authority;
- justification by example; and
- generalizable arguments.

Appeal to Authority

By appealing to authority, children actually avoid mathematical justification. "Mr. Jones told us last year that when you multiply by 10 you just put a zero at the end." A primary goal of mathematics instruction portrayed in this book is to help students understand that they need to question ideas and use mathematical arguments to justify them. Students need to decide for themselves whether something makes sense and not accept something as true just because someone says it is true.

Justification by Example

The most common form of justification used by children in the elementary school is justification by example. In the next example, Ms. V. has asked one of the second-grade students in her class to think about how to prove a conjecture about adding two even numbers. The student, Kimberly, suggests trying a number of examples.

Ms. V.:   Okay, we have a conjecture about adding even numbers: *When you add two even numbers, you get an even number.* How would we show that is always true no matter what even numbers we use?

Kimberly: We could try it.

Ms. V.:   What do you mean we could try it? We could add two even numbers and that would show that it was always true?

Kimberly: No. We could all try it. Everyone in the class could do some. We could each try a lot of numbers.

Ms. V.:   So if we have a lot of numbers, will that show it is always true?

Kimberly: Well, if all the answers were even it would.

Ms. V.: Could you try all the numbers?

Kimberly: No. But you could try a lot of numbers.

Ms. V.: How about the numbers we didn't try? How could we be sure it worked for them?

Kimberly: Well if it works for all the numbers we try, it probably works for the other numbers, too.

Ms. V.: Suppose someone in the class said there might be an even number that we haven't tried that it won't work for?

Kimberly: I'd tell them they had to show me the number.

Kimberly seems to believe that if nobody can find an example that does not work, then the conjecture must be true, or at least the conjecture should be accepted as true until someone can find a counterexample to refute it.

Some children who use examples to justify a conjecture are not themselves convinced that the examples actually justify that the conjecture is true for all numbers. In many cases, the children cannot think of anything else to do. They are, however, beginning to appreciate the need for more general forms of argument, and that provides a basis for engaging students in a search for other forms of justification.

General Forms of Justification

Young children do not commonly use generalizable arguments, but as they move into the intermediate grades they begin to see the limits of arguing by examples and can be encouraged to try to employ more general forms of argument.

Restating the conjecture

As children struggle to find more general forms of justification, some children use arguments in which they essentially restate the conjectures. The conjectures appear so obvious to them that they cannot think of anything that is necessary beyond reiterating the conjecture. For example, Sarah had the following conversation with Ms. V. about her justification for the following conjecture:

When you add two numbers, you can change the order of the numbers you add, and you will still get the same answer.

Sarah: When you add, it doesn't matter which order the numbers are in—you always get the same number, no matter what the numbers are.

Ms. V.: How do you know that is true for all numbers, Sarah?

Sarah: If the numbers don't change, then the answer will be the same.

Ms. V.: Is that always true? How about 8 minus 6 equals 6 minus 8. Is that true?

Sarah: No. It's only true for addition.

Ms. V.: If it is not true for subtraction, how do you know that it is always true for addition?

Sarah: Because you can add numbers in any order. It's always the same.

To Sarah the conjecture seemed obvious. She did not seem to need examples to convince herself that it was true, and she appeared to want to provide an argument that was general. She fell short, however, in that her argument simply restated the conjecture in slightly different words.

Concrete examples that are more than examples: Building on basic concepts

One of the difficulties that elementary school children have in providing arguments that conjectures are true for all numbers is that they often do not have a way of talking about numbers in general or a notation system to represent them. They often have to go back to specific cases. But there are ways of making arguments with specific cases such that the arguments do not depend on the specific numbers. For example, consider how Alicia justified this conjecture:

> *When you add two numbers, you can change the order of the numbers you add, and you will still get the same number.*

Alicia: It's like this. If you have 7 plus 5 [*puts out a set of 7 blocks and to the right of it a set of 5 blocks*], look you can move them like this [*moves the set of 5 blocks so that they are to the left of the set of 7 blocks*]. Now it's 5 plus 7, but it's still the same blocks. It's going to be the same when you count them all. It doesn't matter which you count first; it's still going to be the same.

Ms. P.: Okay, I see how that works for 7 and 5, but how do you know that is true for all numbers?

Alicia: It doesn't matter how many are in the groups. It could be any number. You are just moving them around like I did there; they are still the same blocks no matter what number you use.

Although Alicia used a specific example to justify the conjecture, she did not just calculate the answer. In fact, at no time did she state that $7 + 5 = 12$. She demonstrated a process in which she represented the first sum and transformed that representation to represent the second sum. Upon prompting, she stated that the same process could be used with any numbers. It is important to note that Alicia used a very concrete solution, and it was the concreteness of the representation that allowed her to generalize to all numbers. If she had simply calculated the answer, she would not have been able to generalize from her solution. We usually think of abstract solutions as more sophisticated than solutions involving physical objects, but in this case the more concrete solution provided a basis for generalization. It is critical that students explicitly recognize that the process they have used generalizes to all numbers. To understand this justification, students must also recognize that moving objects in a collection that is being counted does not change the total number of objects. Note that, as it stands, this justification just applies to whole numbers and does not demonstrate that addition of fractions or negative numbers is commutative. However, the same fundamental argument could be used with representations of fractions.

For many of the conjectures listed in Table 4.1, children will need to rely on this type of justification. The following justification that the sum of two odd numbers is even also illustrates this form of argument. There are several ways that young children think about even numbers and odd numbers. One possibility is to make a set representing the given number and partition the set into groups of two. If all the elements of the set can be paired up into groups of two, the number is even. If there is one left over that cannot be paired up, the number is odd. Jamie's justification that *the sum of two odd numbers is even* is based on this definition.

Jamie: Well, for any odd number, you have groups of two with one left over. So the two odd numbers have two leftovers, and you can put them together, so there are no leftovers that are not paired up. So it's even.

Ms. P.: Could you show me with the blocks?

Jamie: See, here is one odd number. [*She makes a collection of pairs of blocks together with one additional block.*] And here is another. [*She makes another collection of pairs of blocks together with one additional block. In both cases she does not bother to count the pairs of blocks, so she does not know how many blocks she has. She only knows that they represent an odd number because there is a block left over.*] Now we put them together, and we still have all these pairs, but now these two pair up with each other. [*She puts the two single blocks together to make another pair.*] See, all the blocks are paired up. So the number is even. (See Figure 7.1.)

Building on already justified conjectures

Some conjectures can be justified using conjectures that have already been justified. For example, all the conjectures about subtraction and division involving zero or 1 in Table 4.1 can be proved by using the relationship between addition and subtraction or the relationship between multiplication and division and using the appropriate conjecture about adding zero or mul-

FIGURE 7.1
Jamie's strategy for showing that the sum of two odd numbers is even.

tiplying by 1. Those proofs will be discussed in Chapter 9. Clearly not all conjectures can be proved using other conjectures. Some conjectures need to serve as basic building blocks that can be used to prove other conjectures. Addition of zero, multiplication by 1, and the commutative properties for addition and multiplication represent conjectures that can be justified only by methods similar to those discussed in the preceding section.

A conjecture that children frequently recognize as related to previously proved conjectures involves adding and subtracting the same number. In the following episode, Pete describes how he justifies that $a + b - b = a$.

Pete: Because b minus b is zero. We know that. That's Conjecture 11 [*pointing to the conjecture posted on the wall that they had already proved*].

Ms. V.:   How does that help you know that this is always true?

Pete: Because we also know that a plus zero is zero. That's Conjecture 4. So we have b minus b equals zero, and that gives us a plus zero equals a, which we also know is true. So that means the conjecture is always true.[1]

---

[1] This justification also makes implicit use of the property $(a + b) - c = a + (b - c)$, but Ms. V. decides to let that go at this point. This and related conjectures about adding and subtracting more than two numbers are discussed in a later chapter.

This example is one that is relatively easy for children to grasp. For many conjectures, however, this method requires a few additional basic definitions and principles that we have not yet introduced. We will discuss such justifications in Chapters 8 and 9.

Children's Use of Counterexamples

Although conjectures cannot be justified as being true for all numbers simply by providing examples, a single counterexample is sufficient to demonstrate that a conjecture is not true for all numbers. If we can find one exception, the conjecture is not true for all numbers. In particular, it is not true for the exception we have found. For example, the conjecture that *an even number divided by an even number is even* is not true for all even numbers. Although many examples are consistent with the conjecture (e.g., $12 \div 2$, $8 \div 2$, $24 \div 6$), it is not true for $6 \div 2$. Although we can find many other pairs of numbers that seem to support the conjecture, the single counterexample establishes that it is not true for all numbers.

Many children by the first and second grade seem to have a reasonable grasp of using counterexamples to show that a conjecture is not true. They frequently use counterexamples to show that a conjecture as stated is not true for all numbers. The example near the beginning of Chapter 4 in which children discussed how to state the conjecture about adding zero illustrates this use of counterexamples.

ADDITIONAL EXAMPLES OF JUSTIFICATION

The arguments that can be used to justify conjectures take different forms for different conjectures. Some conjectures are easier to justify than others are. Some seem so trivial that the justification seems almost like stating the obvious.

Conjectures About Zero and 1

Students' justifications for conjectures about zero and 1 come very close to simply restating the conjecture. Consider the following justification for the conjecture:

When you subtract a number from itself, you get zero ($a - a = 0$).

Eva: Minus means you take that number away from what you had. So if you have 7 minus 7, you have 7 things and you take away all 7 of the things, so you don't have any left. Zero. It's like that for any number. Subtract a number from itself— it means that you have a number of things, and you take away that number of things. That means you take them all away. That leaves you with zero things.

Eva started with a specific example, but then noted that the argument for 7
− 7 could be generalized to any number. The description of the action with
the collections of objects does not seem much different from simply restating the conjecture using concrete referents, but her argument does bring in
what it means to subtract in this particular case.

Juan's justification for the following conjecture provides an additional
example of justification similar to Eva's:

*When you multiply a number times 1, you get the number you started
with ($a \times 1 = a$).*

Juan: A number times 1, that means you have that many groups
with 1 thing in each group, so that gives you that number
of things. Like, you have 9 groups with 1 thing in each
group. So that's 9 things. You can just count the 9 things.
The answer is 9. It's like that for any number.

Commutative Properties

Justifications of the commutative properties for both addition and multiplication involve a little more explicit action than the previous justifications
involving zero and 1. A justification of the commutative property for addition was discussed earlier in this chapter. In that case, the child giving the
justification physically moved the sets to illustrate why addition is commutative. There are some parallels with the way children justify commutativity
for multiplication. A set representing $a \times b$ is transformed so that it becomes
$b \times a$ without changing the objects in the set.

For elementary school children, multiplication involving whole num-
bers ($m \times n$) is often conceived of as m collections with n things in each collection or in terms of an m-by-n array. Justification of the commutative
property for multiplication can be based on either definition, although a
justification based on the array definition may be more transparent than
one based on collections. Following are two justifications for the commutative property of multiplication ($a \times b = b \times a$) The first example uses an array
representation of multiplication.

Sephora: Let's try 7 times 3. [*She makes 7 rows of linking cubes with
3 cubes linked together in each row. Then she makes 3 rows
of linking cubes with 7 cubes linked together in each row.*]
Look, you can put this one on top of this one. [*She takes
the 3 rows of 7 cubes and rotates it 90 degrees and places it
on top of the 7 rows of 3.*] See, it fits.

Ms. M.: How does that show you that you can change the order
of the numbers when you multiply?

Sephora: Because all I did was turn it, and it fit. When I turned
it, it became 7 times 3 instead of 3 times 7. Hey, I didn't

have to make the two groups. I could have just made one and turned it. I could do that with any number, and it would be the same. (See Figure 7.2.)

The second example represents 4 × 5 as 4 groups with 5 things in each group and transforms that to 5 groups with 4 things in each group.

Kevin: It's like this. Say I have 4 times 5. That means I have 4 groups with 5 in each group. [*Makes 4 groups with 5 blocks in each group*] I can make new groups like this. I take one block from each group and make a new group. Since I had 4 groups, there will be 4 in this new group. I take the next block from each set and make another new group. I keep doing that until I have taken all the blocks out of the old groups and made new groups with one block from each [original] group. There were 4 groups, so, there are 4 in each new group, and there were 5 in each [old] group, so there were enough to make 5 groups.

That's 5 times 4. See? And it doesn't matter how many groups I had or how many were in the groups. I would always get new groups that are the same size as the number of groups I started with and the number of new groups I would get would be the same as the number I had in each of the old groups.[2]

Even and Odd Numbers

Justification of conjectures involving even and odd numbers depends on the definition of even and odd numbers that students are using and upon the ways that even and odd numbers are represented. Earlier in the chapter we defined even and odd numbers by partitioning a set representing the given number into groups of two. If all the elements of the set can be paired up into groups of two, the number is even. If there is one left over that cannot be paired up, the number is odd. Proofs involving this basic definition generally follow the same form as the proof illustrated earlier in this chapter. Start with the initial sets grouped by two with or without one left over, depending on whether the number is even or odd. Combine the sets as indicated in the conjecture, keeping the groups of two intact insofar as possible. When possible, pair the extra elements from odd numbers, and examine the results to see whether you can account for all of the elements in pairs or whether there is a leftover element. If all of the objects can be grouped into pairs, the result is even. If there is one leftover element, the result is odd. Consider a proof of another conjecture using the same basic definition. In this case the problem is not actually stated as a conjecture to be justified, but as a problem to be solved. The solution of the problem actually results in a conjecture and its justification.

> *Problem: When you subtract a smaller odd number from an even number, what kind of number do you get for your answer?*

Jamie: Well, you have an even number—it's like this. [*She puts out a number of groups of 2 blocks without bothering to count the total number of groups.*] And you take away an odd number. That means you will take away some number of these [*She removes some groups of 2.*], but you'll also have to take away 1 more, because the odd number has 1 extra. The other 1 will always be a leftover, so it will always be an odd number.

Another example of a justification of a conjecture about multiplication involving even numbers draws on an already proven generalization about adding even numbers.

---

[2]Kevin's justification applies only to whole numbers and cannot be extended to fractions. Sephora's definition also applies only to whole numbers, but her justification could be modified to apply to fractions as well by using an $n \times m$ rectangle.

Conjecture: When you multiply a counting number times an even number, you get an even number.

Rosa: Easy. We know that when you add even numbers you get an even number as the answer. When you multiply a counting number times an even number, it's just like adding a lot of even numbers, so it's even.

Ms. M.: But the conjecture we proved was just about adding two even numbers.

Rosa: Yeah, but it's just the same thing. You add two even numbers, you get an even number. You add that even number to the next even number, and you get another even number. You can keep on doing that no matter how many numbers you add. You're always just adding even numbers. So it doesn't matter how many numbers you have. It's always going to be even.

In later chapters we will consider some additional ways that children can justify conjectures about even and odd numbers by introducing some notation for representing them that makes it possible to use other conjectures in the proofs.

INTERACTIONS ABOUT JUSTIFICATION

To encourage students to think about justification, there are some basic questions that teachers ask repeatedly. Over time students adopt these questions themselves, so that when a conjecture is proposed, the following questions are posed:

- Is that always true?
- How do you know that is true for all numbers?
- Okay, so we have seen that it works for a lot of numbers, but how do we know that there is not some number—maybe a very, very big number—that it will not work for?

TEACHER COMMENTARY 7.1

I want to tell teachers not to get discouraged if at first it is hard for kids to justify conjectures. For one, kids have never done this before; they have never been asked to think this way. Also, teachers have never had to question kids before like this. It will come, but it might take both you and your kids awhile.

In my first year, I didn't seem to get many proofs out; it was hard to move my kids beyond repeated examples. Over time I developed some key questions that really helped, like

"How do you know this will work for all numbers?" and "How do you know this will always be true?" I used to wait until we had a lot of conjectures generated before I even introduced the idea of justification. Now if we come up with a conjecture, we will discuss it and then start working on justifying it. The kids are thinking about the idea of the conjecture, and I like to strike while the iron is hot. I also had to figure out what makes an acceptable proof for kids in third and fourth grade. Now that I have seen what types of proofs kids generate and have discussed these proofs with other teachers, I know what to look for in certain proofs.

I have really struggled with how to get all kids involved in justifying conjectures. It bothered me that some kids didn't participate when we had whole-class discussions. Now I start by having every child write a response to the question, "Why will this conjecture always be true?" Even if some kids write only repeated examples, they are writing about the ideas, and they are active participants. After they are done writing, I put them into groups where they work together on justifying the conjecture. They share their justifications with me and then I have them present their justifications to the class. The other kids can then ask questions to challenge their justification. I ask kids to check to make sure that the justifications are complete and convincing. Finally, after the class discussion, the kids go back to their journals to think about what they initially wrote about this conjecture. They can add to what they had written, they can change it, or they can just leave it. I really saw growth in every child from the first journal entry to the second. Not that every child had a perfect understanding of justification, but rather that they all were able to add something that was a more generalized way of thinking. I have been at this for four years and I really feel that I have a system that works for engaging all my kids in justification.

Mary Bostrom, Third- and fourth-grade teacher

Discussing the Justification of *a + b − b = a*

Following is a discussion with a second-grade student as she attempts to justify the conjecture $a + b - b = a$. The student starts out with what she describes as using examples. But as she does the calculation, she uses knowledge about subtracting a number from itself and about adding zero to a number. Her initial strategy of operating on numbers does not depend on the specific numbers she chooses; she essentially is treating the numbers as variables. In other words, she actually uses properties that she could use in a more general proof, and that is what Ms. L. leads her to see. Note the decisions Ms. L. makes about when to intervene and what questions she asks to draw Susie out.

Susie has been in a class that spends quite a lot of time discussing conjectures and how students know that a given conjecture is true for all numbers. The class also has talked about numbers that usually are not encountered in the second grade, and Susie chooses both fractions and negative numbers for her examples.

Ms. L.:   Here's a conjecture. [$a + b - b = a$] First of all I want you to look at it and tell me if you think that it is a true conjecture.

Susie: It says *a* plus *b* minus *b* equals *a*. I think it's true.

Ms. L.:   Do you think it's always true?

Susie: Probably.

Ms. L   How could you show that that was always true?

Susie: Well, if you used all the numbers it would take forever, but if I used one of each type of number, it might prove it. Fractions, regular numbers, negative numbers, really high numbers, really low numbers.

Although Susie proposes to justify the conjecture by trying examples, she still shows a lot of insight. She recognizes that she cannot try all the numbers, and she also recognizes that she should try a variety of numbers. Although this strategy does not prove that the conjecture holds for all numbers, it could help Susie figure out whether or not it is likely that the conjecture is true. Trying a variety of different types of numbers is a good strategy for finding counterexamples. If she could find one counterexample, she would know the conjecture is not true for all numbers. If she cannot find any counterexamples, she would have more confidence that the conjecture is true, even though she could not be sure.

Ms. L.:   Okay. Hold it for a second, Susie. [*Susie is starting to compute and Ms. L. stops her.*] So you're saying, if you were going to try out numbers, you would try out different types of numbers?

Susie: Yeah.

Ms. L.:   So is that how you would show that's always true? Would you just try all those different numbers? Is that what you would do?

Susie: Probably. That's one of the ways you could do it.

Ms. L.:   Okay. And if it worked for all the numbers, then what would you—

Susie: [*Interrupting*] All the different types. Then I could say, I think this would always be true.

Ms. L.:   Would you be sure?

Susie: Pretty sure.

Ms. L.:   Oh? Why not completely sure?

Susie: Because you haven't tried every number, but you can't do every number.

Ms. L.:   So is there any way to show this is always true, since you can't do every number because you can't spend forever doing it?

Susie: Well, you might be able to do a number sentence and put in different numbers each time, but not all the numbers, different types.

Ms. L: Okay. I understand that and I think that if we sat down, I could see you try it with different types of numbers. Is there anything else that you could do?

Susie: Not that I can think of.

Ms. L.:   So what do you want to do now?

Susie: I could try to prove it by doing all different types.

Ms. L.:   Okay.

Susie recognizes the limitations of trying different numbers. She thinks that if it works for a lot of different numbers, the conjecture probably is true, but she understands that she would not be absolutely sure that it is true for all numbers. Ms. L. has attempted to get Susie to consider alternative ways of justifying the conjecture, but at this general level of discussion, Susie can think only about trying different examples. Ms. L. decides to let Susie try several examples.

Susie: We can start with fractions, fractions plus low and high numbers and things like that.

Ms. L.:   Wow! That's going to be a lot of different numbers to try. Why don't you go through one of them, okay?

Susie: [*Writes* $\frac{1}{2} + 11 - 11 =$] Eleven . . . well, if you have 11 and you take away 11, it will get you zero. So it's like $\frac{1}{2}$ equals $\frac{1}{2}$. [*Writes* $\frac{1}{2}$ *after the = sign*]

Although Susie has worked through an example with specific numbers, the way she has carried out the calculation suggests that she has insight as to why the conjecture is true for all numbers. She does not simply calculate from left to right. She subtracts 11 from 11 to get zero and then adds zero to $\frac{1}{2}$. As becomes evident in the next two examples, she is not really calculating. She is using two basic properties to carry out the calculation ($b - b = 0$, and $a + 0 = a$). Although she is using specific numbers, it does not matter what the numbers are. The numbers act like variables. In the examples that follow, Susie makes explicit her understanding of these properties and how she is using them.

Susie: I'm going to try some other numbers. Like I could do negative 5 plus 5 minus 5 equals. [*Writes* $-5 + 5 - 5 =$] Five take away 5 again will get you to zero and that would leave a negative 5 that you started with. Yep, that's true.

Ms. L.:   Okay.

Susie: Now you could do the opposite thing and have the positive 5 and the negative 5 minus the negative 5. [*Writes*

$5 + -5 - -5 = $] Well, the negative 5 minus the negative 5 will get you to zero again.

Ms. L.: Okay. How do you know that?

Susie: I just know if you have a number and you minus the same number it gets you to zero. So it's got to be 5. [*Writes = 5*]

Ms. L.: Okay. So let me see if I understand this, Susie. What did you say? If you have a number and you minus the same number, it gets you to zero.

Susie: Yeah. And then zero plus any other number will equal the number you started with.

Ms. L.: And any number plus zero is itself?

Susie: Yeah. So those two conjectures make up this conjecture. So we have, like, two conjectures put together. [*Points to the original conjecture*]

By asking Susie to explain how she knows that negative 5 minus negative 5 gives zero, Ms. L. encourages Susie to make explicit the property she is using. Susie responds with the general property about subtracting a number from itself and then volunteers that this property together with the property about adding zero make up the conjecture she is trying to prove. In order to give Susie the chance to consolidate her knowledge and make explicit what she has said, Ms. L. next asks Susie to show her what she just said using variables.

Ms. L.: I'm going to rewrite that conjecture here for you because I want you to do some circling for me. So we have *a* plus *b* minus *b* equals *a*. Could you circle the conjectures you're talking about here? I think I understand what you're saying, but I want it to be real clear.

Susie: This is one conjecture. [*Circles b − b and writes = 0 inside the circle*]

Ms. L.: And what is that conjecture?

Susie: This conjecture would be *A number minus a number equals zero*. Well, if it's the same number.

Ms. L.: Okay. Are these the same number?

Susie: Yes. Because of the mathematicians' rule of repeated variables. If you put two variables in the problem that are the same, they have to be the same thing.

Ms. L.: All right. So here's one of your conjectures: *b* minus *b* equals zero.

Susie: Yeah.

Ms. L.: Then you said there was another conjecture in there?

Susie: Yeah.

Ms. L.:   What's that?

Susie: This plus this. [*Draws a loop around $a + 0$ and writes $= a$ inside the loop* (see Figure 7.3).]

Ms. L.:   Oh. Now Susie, does what you just told me about the two conjectures—does that prove that this conjecture up here is always true?

Susie: Well, if the other two are true, then it would be true.

This comment shows a lot of insight. Susie recognizes that her proof depends on the fact that the two properties she has used are true for all numbers.

Ms. L.:   Oh, okay. Let's say that we've already proved that *b* minus *b* equals zero is always true, and *a* plus zero equals *a* is always true. Then what?

Susie: That would prove this is true. [*Pointing to $a + b - b = a$*]

Ms. L.:   Wow! Very nice, Susie. Which is better: trying different numbers or this way? [*Pointing to what Susie has just done*]

Susie: This way because it would take your whole life and you still wouldn't have found out the numbers. This way you only have to do one thing and you've proved it.

Ms. L.:   For all numbers?

Susie: Yeah.

Ms. L.:   Very nice!

FIGURE 7.3
Photo of Susie's Work

Very nice indeed! Susie started out proposing to justify the conjecture by trying examples. If Ms. L. had taken her initial comments at face value, she might have missed the opportunity for Susie to show what she understood. By letting Susie work through examples, by listening to Susie's explanations, and by asking Susie to justify what she was doing, Ms. L. was able to help Susie build on what she knew to come up with a general justification of the conjecture. In the process Susie not only solved the given problem but also appeared to learn a great deal about what is involved in proving a conjecture.

A CAVEAT

Many younger children may not be able to generate or even follow some of the forms of argument we have discussed in this chapter. We believe, however, that it is productive for young children to generate conjectures, even when they cannot prove them in a general sense. Children tend to be able to generate conjectures and use conjectures in meaningful ways well before they are able to understand what constitutes appropriate justification. We also have found that it is productive to ask children whether their conjectures are always true and how they know that they are always true for all numbers. Although most children in the primary grades may not provide general arguments to support their conjectures, the interactions around these questions can produce some interesting discussion and yield some interesting insights about children's thinking. Asking these questions also lays the groundwork for developing ideas of justification in more depth in later grades.

We are reluctant to provide guidelines about the grade levels at which certain kinds of thinking emerge in children. We consistently have been surprised at what children are capable of when given the opportunity. The following observations should be taken as provisional and not assumed to be true for all children or all classes. With those qualifications, we will share our observations.

We have found that most first- and second-grade children rely on justification by example. We have, however, observed some classrooms in which first- and second-grade children have generated some very nice justifications for their conjectures. Although many first- and second-grade children do not readily generate spontaneous justifications for their conjectures, a number of them do begin to appreciate the limits of justification by example, so they are beginning to struggle with the need for more general forms of justification. Although many first- and second-grade students will have difficulty producing general arguments about why they think a conjecture is true for all numbers, questioning them encourages students to think about how to show that conjectures are true. Furthermore, some primary-grade students, like Susie in the example earlier, do offer valid general arguments.

By the third or fourth grade, a number of children can begin to use and/or understand more general forms of argument. We have found that many children at this age appreciate more general forms of argument even when they are not able to generate them themselves. A few of them are capable of using quite abstract notation to represent their justifications. By the fifth and sixth grades, it is possible to engage a class in quite sophisticated discussions of justification.

CHALLENGES

1. What kind of number do you get when you add three odd numbers? Can you justify your response?
2. How would you justify that $a \times b \div b = a$ (provided that b does not equal zero)?
3. What kind of questions do you think might help children see the limitations of justifying by example?
4. What kind of questions might help students think about ways that they might justify that addition is commutative?
5. What kind of questions might help students think about ways that they might justify that multiplication is commutative?
6. Choose a conjecture that your class has generated and describe different ways that children might justify that this conjecture is always true.
7. Using the same conjecture as in Challenge 6, ask your students how they could show that this conjecture is always true. Did their justifications match the ones you described in Challenge 6?

8 | ORDERING MULTIPLE OPERATIONS

In previous chapters, most of the discussion has focused on conjectures about operations on just two numbers. In this chapter we consider cases in which more than two numbers are added, subtracted, multiplied, and/or divided. There are two fundamental properties that provide us some flexibility in dealing with addition and multiplication when more than two numbers are added or multiplied. There also is an important property that connects addition and multiplication. Finally there is the question of what order to carry out calculations when there is more than one operation in a number sentence.

In the previous chapters, we focused on ideas that students frequently generate themselves and how those ideas might emerge in class discussion. This chapter differs somewhat from those earlier chapters. We consider properties of number operations that are somewhat less intuitive for many students and can be more difficult to justify. We also consider how students implicitly use these basic properties and others in their calculations. We do not expect that students will make explicit the properties they use as they compute in the detail that we provide in this chapter, but we believe that it is important to understand the mathematics underlying students' thinking and the procedures they use. Because of these considerations, the discussion in this chapter focuses a bit more on mathematics content than did previous chapters.

THE ASSOCIATIVE PROPERTY OF ADDITION

It is so common for students to add more than two numbers that they seldom explicitly think about how they are grouping numbers in order to add them. In fact, most students do not think about the fact that they actually are adding numbers two at a time. As a consequence, they often do not come up with a specific conjecture about how they can group numbers to add three or more of them, and it often takes some effort to get students to recognize the following basic property of addition involving three or more numbers.

Associative Property of Addition: When you add three numbers, it does not matter whether you start by adding the first pair of numbers or the last pair of numbers.

This can be represented symbolically as $(a + b) + c = a + (b + c)$ for all numbers a, b, and c.

Following is an example of a classroom interaction in which the class discusses a number sentence designed to make the associative property of addition an explicit focus of attention. In the process of discussing this example, it becomes necessary to have a notation to make explicit which numbers are being added first, so the teacher introduces parentheses as a notation to show the order in which calculations are carried out. The open number sentence the students are working on is 56 + 75 + 25 = ☐. Grouping 75 and 25 together makes the calculation quite a bit easier than starting with 56 + 75, but some students routinely begin calculating at the left of the expression.

Eric: I got 156.

Ms. L.: How did you get that?

Eric: I added 56 and 75. Fifty and 70, that's 120, and 6 and 5 is 11. Then 11 and 120 is 131. And I added 25 to that and got 156.

Ms. L.: Any questions for Eric? [*Pause to wait for students to respond*] Did anyone do it a different way?

Sarah: I added the 75 and 25 first because I knew that was 100. So it was just 56 plus 100.

Ms. L.: Why did you do that?

Sarah: Because it's a lot easier that way. I know 75 and 25, and then I'm just adding 100.

Ms. L.: Is it okay to do that?

Sarah: Yeah. I'm still adding all the same numbers.

Ms. L.: So what is the difference between the way that Eric solved the problem and the way that Sarah solved it?

Roger: Eric added the 56 and 75 first, and Sarah added the 75 and 25 first.

Ms. L.: Let me show you a way to write that. When mathematicians want to group numbers together to show how they want to combine them, they use parentheses. Here is how they would show what Eric did. [*Ms. L. writes (56 + 75) + 25 = 156.*] And here is how they would write what Sarah did. [*Ms. L writes 56 + (75 + 25) = 156.*] Eric and Sarah added the numbers differently, but they both got the same answer. Does anyone want to say anything about this?

The discussion continues. The class looks at several similar examples and uses parentheses to distinguish between the different solutions. After some discussion, the class comes up with a conjecture about the associative property of addition.

To show that the conjecture about the associative property is true for all whole numbers, students might use an argument somewhat similar to the argument used for the commutative property:

Tyrone: If I had this *[points to (4 + 7) + 9]*, I could make it like this. *[Tyrone joins together a collection of 4 red linking cubes, to the right of that a collection of 7 yellow linking cubes, and to the right of that a collection of 9 blue linking cubes]* And if I was adding the 4 and 7 first, I would put these together *[joining the red and yellow linking cubes]*, and then I would put these *[indicating the set of 9 blue linking cubes]* with them *[joining the blue linking cubes to the yellow cubes]*. If I were doing it the other way *[points to 4 + (7 + 9) and breaks the cubes he has joined into the original collections]*, I would put these together first *[joining together the yellow and blue linking cubes]*, and then I would put this with them *[joining the 4 red linking cubes to the yellow linking cubes]*. Either way I would end up counting the same blocks. It doesn't matter which ones I put together first. I still have all the same blocks in the end, so it will be the same number. It would be like that for any numbers. (See Figure 8.1.)

FIGURE 8.1
The Associative Property of Addition

THE ASSOCIATIVE PROPERTY OF MULTIPLICATION

Although it is more common to add more than two numbers than it is to multiply more than two numbers, we also can multiply three or more numbers. Just as we found parallels between other properties of addition and corresponding properties of multiplication, multiplication is also associative.

> *Associative Property of Multiplication: When you multiply three numbers, it does not matter whether you start by multiplying the first pair of numbers or the last pair of numbers.*

This can be represented symbolically as $(a \times b) \times c = a \times (b \times c)$ *for all numbers a, b, and c.*

It is not likely that, on their own, students will come up with a justification for the associative property of multiplication, but the property can be illustrated with a three-dimensional array, as shown in Figure 8.2.

Subtraction and Division

As was the case with the commutative property, neither subtraction nor division is associative. This is not entirely intuitive for many students, but almost any selection of numbers will provide a counterexample.

$$(12 - 7) - 3 = 2 \quad \text{but} \quad 12 - (7 - 3) = 8$$
$$(48 \div 6) \div 2 = 4 \quad \text{but} \quad 48 \div (6 \div 2) = 16$$

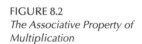

FIGURE 8.2
The Associative Property of Multiplication

In the first subtraction example, both the 7 and the 3 are subtracted from 12. In the second example, the 3 is subtracted from the number that is going to be subtracted from 12. In the first case, subtracting 3 makes the final answer smaller. In the second, it makes the number that will be taken away from 12 smaller, which actually makes the final answer larger.

THE DISTRIBUTIVE PROPERTY

Another fundamental property, called the *distributive property of multiplication over addition*, relates addition and multiplication.

> *Distributive Property of Multiplication over Addition: When you multiply a number n times the sum of two numbers, you can add the two numbers first and then multiply n times this sum, or you can multiply n times each number to be added and then add the results of these calculations.*
>
> *This can be represented symbolically as $a \times (b + c) = (a \times b) + (a \times c)$ or alternatively as $(b + c) \times a = (b \times a) + (c \times a)$.*

As is the case for most properties involving multiplication, this property is most clearly shown using an array representation of multiplication. The array in Figure 8.3 can be thought of as representing either $6 \times (3 + 5)$ or $(6 \times 3) + (6 \times 5)$.

Subtraction and Division

Multiplication does distribute over subtraction. Symbolically, this can be represented as:

$a \times (b - c) = (a \times b) - (a \times c)$ for all a, b, and c.

Or alternatively as

$(b - c) \times a = (b \times a) - (c \times a)$ for all a, b, and c.

The situation is more complex for division:

$(b + c) \div a = (b \div a) + (c \div a)$ for all numbers except $a = 0$.

But it is *not* true that $a \div (b + c) = (a \div b) + (a \div c)$.

$24 \div (4 + 2) = 24 \div 6 = 4$ *but* $(24 \div 4) + (24 \div 2) = 6 + 12 = 18$

FIGURE 8.3
The Distributive Property of Multiplication over Addition

STUDENTS' IMPLICIT UNDERSTANDING AND USE OF BASIC PROPERTIES

When students use relational thinking to transform expressions to simplify calculations, they are applying basic properties of number operations. At the beginning of Chapter 7 we looked at three examples of students using relational thinking to change computational exercises so that the computation would be easier or so they could apply what they already knew. Although these students were implicitly using basic properties, they did not make them explicit. In this section we reconsider these examples and look specifically at the basic properties that underlie these students' strategies. We are not proposing that students be held accountable for justifying each of their steps in transforming an expression. That would be unnecessarily tedious. But it is valuable for us as teachers to appreciate the mathematics underlying their thinking. This gives us insight to recognize the depth of thinking that a student has used, to possibly call attention to a particularly important step in a student's work, or to identify why a proposed procedure is not valid. It also helps us to appreciate how central these basic properties are in the study of arithmetic and algebra.

In the first example, Ali used relational thinking to simplify the calculations to find the number that makes this a true number sentence: $56 + 47 = 54 + d$.

>**Ali:** Fifty-six is two more than 54, so we take the 2 and put it with the 47. That makes 49; so d has to be 49.

Although Ali did not use this notation, his solution could be represented as:

$$56 + 47 = (54 + 2) + 47 = 54 + (2 + 47) = 54 + 49.$$

In this example, Ali implicitly used the associative property of addition to figure out the answer.

In the second example, Kelly figured out that $6 \times 7 = 42$ by relating it to a number fact that she already knew.

>**Kelly:** I know that 5 times 7 is 35 and 6 times 7 is just 5 times 7 and 7 more $[6 \times 7 = 5 \times 7 + 7]$. So it's 35 and 7. That's 42.

This can be represented as in Figure 8.4.[1]

In this example, Kelly used the distributive property and the property involving multiplication by 1 together with some known number facts. She also used additional properties to add $35 + 7$. We will take a more in-depth look at what might be involved in this addition in the next example.

$$
\begin{aligned}
\text{a. } 6 \times 7 &= (5 + 1) \times 7 \\
\text{b. } &= 5 \times 7 + 1 \times 7 \\
\text{c. } &= 5 \times 7 + 7 \\
\text{d. } &= 35 + 7 \\
\text{e. } &= 42
\end{aligned}
$$

FIGURE 8.4
Discrete Steps in Kelly's Relational Thinking About Number Facts

---

TEACHER COMMENTARY 8.1

We were operating at a certain level with mathematics, and now this algebra piece gets us to look at understanding in a bigger way. There are things I don't understand. I am a learner along with my students. Most of us teachers don't use the invented algorithms that the kids

---

[1] The notation used in this example shows that each expression is transformed to the one below it based on a basic property of number operations, a basic computation, and/or the relation between compact and expanded notation for base ten numbers. Because equality is transitive ($a = b$ and $b = c$ implies that $a = c$), all the expressions are equal. In particular the first expression is equal to the last, which is what we are trying to justify.

do. Teachers who don't have a broad understanding of mathematics might end up restricting kids who are thinking outside of the box. I saw a teacher ask a child to solve 20×64. The child said, "It will be easier if 20 is 4 times 5, then I can find what 5 64s are then add that 4 times." The teacher wasn't sure if this would work.

I tell teachers, You need to be comfortable with feeling uncomfortable. As a teacher, I need to think about how I can pose questions like, "Will this work with all numbers?" and "Why is this working?"—questions both for myself and for the students. In order to understand the strategies the kids are using and why they will always work, we need to understand the distributive property. For us teachers, this understanding really has to be grounded so that we can help kids develop these strategies.

Jim Brickweddle, First- and second-grade teacher

Invented Algorithms

As noted in the last chapter, letting students derive and explain procedures for carrying out multidigit calculations can provide an opportunity for students to think about and apply knowledge of fundamental properties of number operations. When students construct their own procedures for adding, subtracting, multiplying, and dividing, the properties that underlie the procedures are close to the surface. Although we would not expect students to justify their steps in the detail that we do here, using and explaining invented procedures like Marta's provides a context for students to think about properties that justify the ways they have manipulated numbers. In order to add two multidigit numbers efficiently, it is necessary to transform the calculation into simpler calculations involving one-digit number facts that have been committed to memory or can be easily generated. These transformations often are not obvious, and in the following discussion we unpack what underlies the transformations that Marta made in carrying out her calculations. Consider Marta's strategy for adding 56 + 39.

Marta: Well, 5 and 3 is 8.

Ms. L.: [*Interrupting*] Where are the 5 and 3?

Marta: Okay, it's 50 and 30. That's like 5 tens and 3 tens. So it's 8 tens; that's 80. And 80 and 6 is 86, and 4 more is 90, and 5 more onto that is 95.

If we were to attempt to represent in some detail the steps that are tied to specific properties that underlie Marta's thinking in this example, it might look like Figure 8.5. Marta starts out by breaking the 56 and 39 into multiples of ten and one. Thus, Step a involves relating representations of base ten numbers in compact and expanded notation. This is the first step in breaking the numbers down in order to add multiples of ten and one. Step b involves the grouping of numbers in order to add tens and ones. Note that this step involves several applications of the associative property

a. $56 + 39 = (5 \times 10 + 6) + (3 \times 10 + 9)$
b. $= (5 \times 10 + 3 \times 10) + (6 + 9)$
c. $= (5 + 3) \times 10 + (6 + 9)$
d. $= 8 \times 10 + (6 + 9)$
e. $= 80 + (6 + 9)$
f. $= (80 + 6) + 9$
g. $= 86 + 9$
h. $= 86 + (4 + 5)$
i. $= (86 + 4) + 5$
j. $= 90 + 5$
k. $= 95$

FIGURE 8.5
*Discrete Steps in Marta's
Invented Procedure for
Adding*

together with the commutative property. In Step c, the distributive property is used so that a number fact $(5 + 3)$ can be used to calculate the sum of multiples of ten. In Steps f and i, the associative property of addition is used in order to group numbers so that 6 can be added to 80 and 4 can be added to the 86 to make 90. Throughout the proof, Marta makes use of specific knowledge about number combinations $(9 = 4 + 5, 86 + 4 = 90, \text{etc.})$.

As students like Marta invent strategies similar to the one just discussed, they are implicitly using basic number properties. They undoubtedly are not aware of the involvement of all the properties that we see in this expanded example, but they probably recognize they are regrouping and reordering the numbers that they are combining. This kind of number sense provides a basis for students to understand computation in the elementary grades and gives them a foundation for generalizing these basic principles to deal with algebraic expressions and equations. For additional discussion of these ideas, see Schifter (1999).

Comparison with the addition algorithm

The commonly used algorithms for adding, subtracting, multiplying, and dividing multidigit numbers depend on these same properties. Because the algorithms are designed for efficiency, the underlying properties are not apparent in the manipulations of numbers involved in carrying out the calculations. Thus, although students routinely use the commutative, associative, and distributive properties when they carry out a standard algorithm, most of them are not aware that they are doing so. For example, in using the addition algorithm, students generally fail to recognize that adding the numbers in the ones column and then adding the numbers in the tens column involves a great deal of regrouping and reordering based on the associative and commutative properties and that adding the numbers in the tens column draws on the distributive property. If we unpack what is going on when students apply the algorithm to a simple calculation involving two-digit numbers, we can see that there is a lot underlying the calculations and that virtually all the steps can be justified using the same basic properties we used to justify the invented procedure for adding two numbers (see Figure 8.6).

FIGURE 8.6
Steps Involved in Adding Two Two-Digit Numbers

$$35$$
$$+\ 48$$

a. $35 + 48 \ = (3 \times 10 + 5) + (4 \times 10 + 8)$

b. $\qquad\qquad = (3 \times 10 + 4 \times 10) + (5 + 8)$

c. $\qquad\qquad = (3 + 4) \times 10 + (5 + 8)$

d. $\qquad\qquad = (5 + 8) + (3 + 4) \times 10$

e. $\qquad\qquad = 13 + (3 + 4) \times 10$

f. $\qquad\qquad = (1 \times 10 + 3) + (3 + 4) \times 10$

g. $\qquad\qquad = (3 + 1 \times 10) + (3 + 4) \times 10$

h. $\qquad\qquad = 3 + (1 \times 10 + (3 + 4) \times 10)$

i. $\qquad\qquad = 3 + (1 + (3 + 4)) \times 10$

j. $\qquad\qquad = 3 + (8 \times 10)$

k. $\qquad\qquad = (8 \times 10) + 3$

l. $\qquad\qquad = 83$

Steps a, f, and l Figure 8.6 involve relating representations of base ten numbers in compact and expanded notation. This is the first step in thinking about adding the numbers in the ones column and the numbers in the tens column. Steps b and c essentially correspond to lining the numbers up so that the 5 is over the 8 and the 3 is over the 4. Note that Step b involves several applications of the associative property together with the commutative property. Step d is required to begin adding in the ones column. Steps f, g, h, and i correspond to carrying the 1 from the 13 to the tens column. We leave it as a challenge to identify the specific properties corresponding to the steps that do not involve number facts or the relation between compact and expanded base ten notation.

Our goal here is not to propose that students actually carry out the calculations at the level of detail depicted in Figures 8.5 and 8.6, but it is interesting to observe how complex the calculations really are and how much work is carried by the notation. It also is noteworthy that the steps in the algorithm can be justified based on a small number of properties of number operations. There is nothing magic about the algorithm. It is simply a very elegant and efficient way of applying these properties. One value of having students devise and discuss alternative procedures for carrying out these calculations is that the properties are closer to the surface in the invented algorithms than they are in the standard algorithm. If students can relate standard algorithms to invented algorithms, they may have more insight into the basic number properties underlying the more streamlined computational algorithms.

Multiplication procedures

Whereas invented procedures for addition and subtraction prominently feature the commutative and associative properties, the distributive property of multiplication over addition plays the central role in multiplying multidigit numbers. Many students implicitly recognize the need to multiply both the tens and ones when multiplying by a single-digit number. Consider the following procedure that a student used to multiply 6×37:

Roger: First I did 6 times 30; that's 180. Then I had to do the 6 times the 7, and that gave me 42 more. So I put them together and I got 222.

Symbolically this can be represented as shown in Figure 8.7.

a. $6 \times 37 \quad = 6 \times (30 + 7)$
b. $\qquad = (6 \times 30) + (6 \times 7)$
c. $\qquad = 180 + 42 = 222$

FIGURE 8.7
Using the Distributive Property in Multiplying

The distributive property is used multiple times when multiplying larger numbers. In the example in Figure 8.8, involving the multiplication of two two-digit numbers, the distributive property is used three times to generate the four partial products. As was the case with the example in Figure 8.6, a number of steps are entailed in actually calculating the partial products and adding them together. We omit these steps to focus on the application of the distributive property.

a. $48 \times 37 \quad = (40 + 8) \times 37$
b. $\qquad = (40 \times 37) + (8 \times 37)$
c. $\qquad = (40 \times (30 + 7)) + (8 \times (30 + 7))$
d. $\qquad = (40 \times 30) + (40 \times 7) + (8 \times 30) + (8 \times 7)$

Exactly the same process is used in algebra to multiply two binomials. The example in Figure 8.9 includes more detail than was provided for multiplying whole numbers, but the critical steps involving the distributive property are the same. Steps a and b involve three applications of the distributive property. In Steps c and d, the terms are reordered and regrouped using the commutative property of multiplication and several applications of the associative property of addition. In Step e, the distributive property is used once again. The final expression is commonly written using traditional algebraic notation as $y^2 + 12y + 35$.

a. $(y + 7) \times (y + 5) \quad = (y \times (y + 5)) + (7 \times (y + 5))$
b. $\qquad = (y \times y + y \times 5) + (7 \times y + 7 \times 5)$
c. $\qquad = (y \times y + 5 \times y) + (7 \times y + 7 \times 5)$
d. $\qquad = y \times y + (5 \times y + 7 \times y) + 7 \times 5$
e. $\qquad = (y \times y) + (5 + 7) \times y + (7 \times 5)$
f. $\qquad = (y \times y) + (12 \times y) + 35$

FIGURE 8.9
Discrete Steps in Multiplying Two Binomials

As illustrated in this example, the distributive property comes into play whenever we add two expressions involving the same variable: $9a + 3a = 9 \times a + 3 \times a = (9 + 3) \times a = 12 \times a$ or $12a$. This is essentially the same thing that we do when we use single-digit number facts to add multiples of ten: $90 + 30 = (9 \times 10) + (3 \times 10) = (9 + 3) \times 10 = 12 \times 10 = 120$.

Because many high school algebra students fail to recognize that simplifying expressions such as $9a + 3a$ involves specific properties of number operations, they often attempt to simplify other expressions in inappropriate ways, such as $7d + 5e = 12de$. This common error, which is made by many beginning algebra students, occurs because students do not appreciate that manipulations of numbers and algebraic symbols depend on fundamental properties of number and number operations.

Although students often are reasonably successful in using the distributive property to multiply a multidigit number by a one-digit number, they often have difficulty recognizing how to use it in multiplying two-digit numbers or binomials. Frequently they tend to just multiply the corresponding digits of each number or the corresponding terms of each binomial. This results in the following types of errors:

$$37 \times 54 = (30 + 7) \times (50 + 4) = (30 \times 50) + (7 \times 4)$$
$$(a + 7)(a + 4) = a^2 + 28$$

In both of these examples, the students have simply multiplied the first and last terms. The algebra error is prevalent when students have learned an algorithm for multiplying multidigit numbers without understanding. Because the distributive property is not at all apparent in the traditional multiplication algorithms, students have little basis for anticipating how the procedures they have learned to multiply whole numbers apply to algebra.

USING THE ASSOCIATIVE AND
DISTRIBUTIVE PROPERTIES IN PROOF

The associative and distributive properties provide some extra tools to construct proofs using mathematical notation. This is particularly useful for most proofs involving even and odd numbers. To illustrate these proofs, we first need to agree on a more formal way of representing even and odd numbers than we used in previous chapters. Because even numbers are divisible by 2, even numbers can be represented in the form $2 \times n$, where n is a whole number. Any positive even number can be represented by this expression, and this expression always represents an even number. Thus, $2 \times n$, where n is a whole number, provides us with a general representation of even numbers. Each odd number is one more than an even number, so odd numbers can be represented in the form $2 \times n + 1$, where n is a whole number. We can use this notation to justify conjectures about even and odd numbers. Following are two examples:

Show that when you multiply an even number times any whole number, you get an even number.

Proof: Let $2 \times n$ be any even number, and m any whole number. The product of an even number times a whole number can therefore be represented by $(2 \times n) \times m$. Using the associative property of multiplication, we can rewrite this as $2 \times (n \times m)$. Multiplying two whole numbers gives a whole number, so $n \times m$ is a whole number. This shows that $2 \times (n \times m)$ is an even number, which completes our proof.

Show that when you add two odd numbers, you get an even number.

Proof: Let $2 \times n + 1$ be one odd number and $2 \times m + 1$ be the second odd number. (Note that we have to choose different variables [m and n] to represent the two odd numbers to cover the most general case. A common error is to use the same variable for both odd numbers. This limits the case to adding an odd number to itself.) The sum of two odd numbers can now be represented as $(2 \times n + 1) + (2 \times m + 1)$. The steps in the proof are given in Figure 8.10. Justification for the individual steps is left as a challenge.

a. $(2 \times n + 1) + (2 \times m + 1) = (2 \times n + 2 \times m) + (1 + 1)$
b. $\qquad\qquad\qquad\qquad = (2 \times n + 2 \times m) + 2$
c. $\qquad\qquad\qquad\qquad = (2 \times n + 2 \times m) + 2 \times 1$
d. $\qquad\qquad\qquad\qquad = 2 \times (n + m) + 2 \times 1$
e. $\qquad\qquad\qquad\qquad = 2 \times ((n + m) + 1)$
f. $(n + m) + 1$ is the sum of three whole numbers, so it is a whole number.
g. Thus, we have 2 multiplied by a whole number, which is an even number.

FIGURE 8.10
Proof That the Sum of Two Odd Numbers Is an Even Number

These proofs may seem a bit sophisticated for elementary school children, but this is essentially what students are doing with the blocks when they justify these conjectures. It is unlikely that many students will adopt this level of formality, but in Figure 8.11 we share a justification for the conjecture about multiplying a whole number by an even number that was produced by one fourth-grade student. He had not learned to use parentheses to show grouping, so he circled the numbers he intended to group. We have edited and reorganized his work a little to make it easier to follow, but the essential ideas were his.

FIGURE 8.11
Steve's Justification

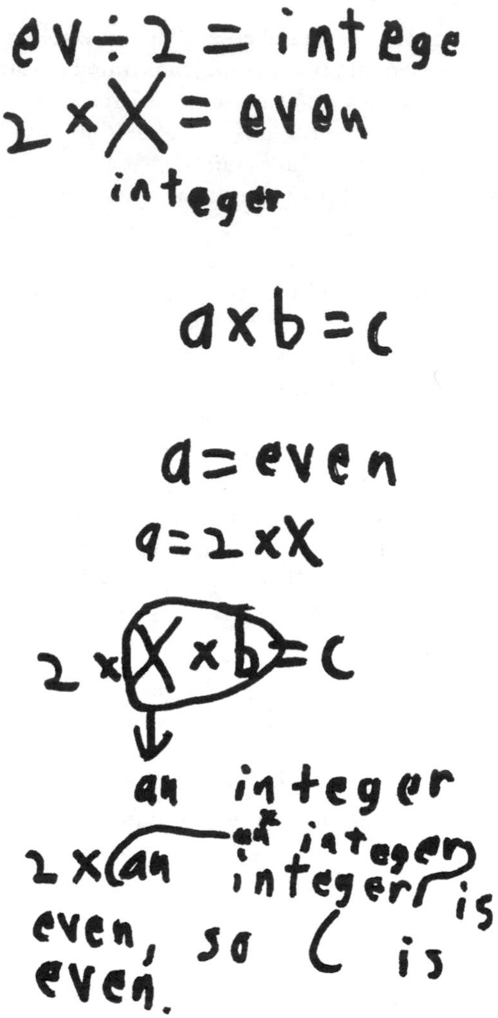

$$ev \div 2 = intege$$
$$2 \times X = even$$
$$integer$$

$$a \times b = c$$

$$a = even$$

$$a = 2 \times X$$

$$2 \times \boxed{X \times b} = c$$

$$an \ integer$$

$$2 \times (an \ integer) \ is$$
$$even, \ so \ c \ is$$
$$even.$$

ORDER OF OPERATIONS

The associative and distributive properties provide guidelines for dealing with specific cases in which more than one operation appears in a number sentence. But how about all the other options for combining operations? What about $3 + 5 \times 7$? Should we add first? Should we multiply first? Does it make a difference? We can easily see that in this case it does make a difference.

$$(3 + 5) \times 7 = 8 \times 7 = 56 \quad but \quad 3 + (5 \times 7) = 3 + 35 = 38$$

We clearly need some rules for deciding what operation to carry out first. One easy solution would be to include parentheses when there is more than a single operation. But what if there are not parentheses; what order should we follow then? We need to agree on a convention so that everyone interprets number sentences in the same way. There are a variety of conventions that we could adopt. The important consideration is that everyone adopts the same convention. The mathematics community throughout the world has adopted the following conventions:

> When a number sentence includes more than one operation, the operations should be carried out in the following order:
>
> 1. operations inside parentheses (in the order given by the next two rules)
> 2. multiplication and division from left to right
> 3. addition and subtraction from left to right

Following are some examples that illustrate the application of these conventions:

> a. $5 + 6 \times 7 = 5 + 42 = 47$
> b. $7 + 24 \div 3 \times 2 - 5 = 7 + 8 \times 2 - 5 = 7 + 16 - 5 = 18$
> c. $2 \times (6 + 2 \times 4 + 4) \div 3 = 2 \times (6 + 8 + 4) \div 3 = 2 \times 18 \div 3 = 36 \div 3 = 12$

Students' Conceptions of Order of Operations

Worrying about the order of operations does not make a lot of sense until students are comfortable dealing with simple number sentences involving multiplication and division. Before students learn the conventions for order of operations, the most common response is to calculate from left to right. Even after they have been exposed to the conventions for order of operations, many students tend to fall back on calculating from left to right. It seems to be very ingrained from their experiences with reading, and it takes some effort to help students adopt these conventions as their own.

Another problem is that students can become too rigid in applying the rules once they have learned them. One of the reasons that it may be productive to wait until children use the associative and distributive properties before talking about order of operations is to provide students alternatives to calculating in a specific sequence without thinking. The order-of-operation conventions apply in cases where it makes a difference what order the calculations are done in. But there are many cases in which it is possible and perhaps easier to follow a different sequence of calculations. In the following cases, a slightly different sequence can be followed because the answer is the same as it would be if the calculations were carried out following the conventions:

> a. $35 \times 24 \div 12$. It is easier to divide 24 by 12 before multiplying, and the answer is the same as multiplying and dividing from the left.

b. **6 + 8 + 3 × 5.** It does not save any work, but it is possible to add 6 + 8 before multiplying 3 × 5. The answer is the same as multiplying first. What we cannot do is add the 14 or the 8 to the 3 before multiplying.

CHALLENGES

1. Justify each of the steps in Figure 8.6.
2. Justify each of the steps in Figures 8.8 and 8.9.
3. Justify each of the steps in Figure 8.10.
4. Addition is associative, but subtraction is not. How about the following:

   a. Is $(a + b) - c = a + (b - c)$ true for all numbers?
   b. Is $(a - b) + c = a - (b + c)$ true for all numbers?

5. As we shall see in the following chapter, most properties of subtraction and division can be derived from corresponding addition and multiplication properties. On the other hand, most of the addition and multiplication properties in Table 4.1 and those introduced in this chapter cannot be derived from the other properties. They represent the foundation on which arithmetic and algebra are built. Surprisingly, one property in Table 4.1 can be derived from the others. That is the property of multiplication by zero (*For all numbers a*, $a \times 0 = 0$). The proof uses properties that one would not suspect would be used to prove something about zero, and it is unlikely that any students would be able to generate this proof on their own. Many, if not most, of them would find it a real challenge to understand it. But it is an interesting proof that uses forms of argument that are also used to justify properties involving multiplication of positive and negative numbers. The steps in the proof are presented here. Justify why each step is valid using basic properties or properties derived from them.[2]

   a. $a \times 0 = (a \times 0) + 0$
   b. $\qquad = (a \times 0) + (a - a)$
   c. $\qquad = ((a \times 0) + a) - a$
   d. $\qquad = ((a \times 0) + a \times 1)) - a$
   e. $\qquad = (a \times (0 + 1)) - a$
   f. $\qquad = (a \times 1) - a$
   g. $\qquad = a - a$
   h. $\qquad = 0$

---

[2] See Challenge 4 for additional properties.

6. Can you think of additional conjectures about even and odd numbers that you can prove?

7. Can you make a conjecture about the sum of three consecutive whole numbers? Can you prove it?

8. Develop a set of true/false or open number sentences that might encourage your students to make explicit the associative property of addition. What questions might you ask to help students focus on the associative property?

9. Develop a set of true/false or open number sentences that might encourage your students to make explicit the associative property of multiplication. What questions might you ask to help students focus on the associative property?

10. Develop a set of true/false or open number sentences that might encourage your students to make explicit the distributive property. What questions might you ask to help students focus on the distributive property?

11. Try the number sentences that you wrote in Challenge 8, 9, or 10 with your students. What did you learn?

REFERENCE

SCHIFTER, DEBORAH. 1999. "Reasoning About Operations: Early Algebraic Thinking in Grades K–6." In Lee V. Stiff & Frances R. Curcio (Eds.) *Developing Mathematical Reasoning in Grades K–12*, pp. 62–81. Reston, VA: National Council of Teachers of Mathematics.

9

"IF . . . THEN . . ." STATEMENTS

Relations Involving Addition, Subtraction, Multiplication, Division, and Equality

In the previous chapters, we considered properties of number operations that can be expressed using number sentences that are true for all replacements of the variables. Whereas these properties could be expressed with a single number sentence, in this chapter we consider relations that are represented as comparisons between two number sentences. In particular, we examine how subtraction is related to addition and how division is related to multiplication. We also return to equality and observe how equality is preserved when the numbers or expressions on both sides of the equal sign are transformed in the same way. As in the preceding chapter, we are concerned here with examining some of the foundations of the mathematics that elementary students engage with. We are not proposing that this chapter provides a model of mathematical activity for elementary students, but the ideas discussed in this chapter do underlie some of the basic ideas that students encounter in arithmetic and beginning algebra. The ideas that we discuss in this chapter together with the basic properties introduced in previous chapters provide the basis for most of arithmetic and beginning algebra.

RELATING SUBTRACTION TO ADDITION AND DIVISION TO MULTIPLICATION

Addition and Subtraction

Consider the following problems:

There are 9 boys and 12 girls in Ms. Keith's second-grade class. How many children are in the class?

There are 21 children in Ms. Keith's second-grade class. Nine of them are boys. How many girls are in the class?

The two problems describe the same situation. The 21 children in the class consist of two groups, 9 boys and 12 girls. We can generate different problems from this situation depending on whether we know the number of children in each group or whether we know the total number of children and how many children are in one of the groups. The first problem might be solved by adding; the second, by subtracting. The second problem also might be solved by thinking about what number to add to 9 to make 21. These problems illustrate the relation between addition and subtraction. One can think of addition or subtraction problems involving positive numbers in terms of a whole and the two parts that make up the whole.[1] When we add, we are trying to find the number representing the whole; when we subtract, we are trying to find the number representing one of the parts. Young children typically do not have an intuitive understanding of this relationship and it is often appropriate for children to solve addition and subtraction problems before considering this relationship. Because this concept is difficult for young children, you probably don't want to address it until children have developed strategies to solve several types of addition and subtraction problems. It can take some time to help students understand how addition and subtraction are related. In spite of these difficulties, it is important that students do develop a clear understanding of this relationship, which can be formally stated as follows:

The Relation Between Addition and Subtraction

- If $a - b = c$, then $a = c + b$
- If $d + e = f$, then $d = f - e$ and $e = f - d$

Elementary students might use this relation in several commonly encountered contexts. One is in learning number facts. If $5 + 8 = 13$, then $13 - 5 = 8$, and $13 - 8 = 5$. If students learn the addition facts and understand the relation between addition and subtraction, they can quickly generate corresponding subtraction facts. Students often learn fact families, but they do not always appreciate the mathematical basis for them. The learning of number facts can provide one context for students to learn how addition and subtraction are related. At the same time, understanding this relation can make the learning of number facts easier and more robust.

A second context in which students might encounter the relation between addition and subtraction is in solving word problems or open number sentences. For example, consider the following problem:

Cheryl has $16. She needs $34 to buy a basketball. How much more money does she have to save to buy the basketball?

---

[1]Although the physical situation we describe is not easy to relate to operations involving negative numbers, it provides a context for thinking about the numbers that children first encounter in the early elementary grades.

This problem is represented most naturally by the number sentence 16 + □ = 34. Both the word problem and the number sentence could be solved by figuring out what to add to 16 to get 34, but students also could solve the corresponding subtraction problem: 34 − 16 = □. Discussing alternative solutions to problems like this often results in different students offering these two different ways of thinking about the problem. This can provide a good context for discussing the relation between addition and subtraction.

TEACHER COMMENTARY 9.1

My third graders were working on this problem:

Ms. D. had 52 books. She needed some more books. Her mom gave her some books for the classroom and now she has 161 books. How many books did her mom give to her?

Bob and Tyrone both subtracted to solve the problem. When asked if this was a subtraction problem, Bob said it wasn't, but subtraction still worked anyway. They thought subtraction would always work to solve a problem like this and went off to write a conjecture about this idea. They worked independently for several minutes and produced the following:

Bob's Conjecture: If you take any number plus a number and it is true and switch the 161 at the beginning and change the plus to a minus and move the 52 to the middle it equals 109

Tyrone's Conjecture: If we take a plus equation and make it a take away. For example, if we have 37 + 47 = 84, you can turn it into 84 − 37 = 47.

Although I was pleased that they had ventured to write their own conjectures, these conjectures did not describe the general relationship between addition and subtraction. I asked them to look at 45 + 21 = 66 and to explain what the big idea would say about this number sentence. They worked together and came up with 66 − 45 = 21. When they compared these number sentences to their conjectures they saw that the conjectures did not fit with this example. They knew that conjectures were supposed to work for all examples of this idea, and so they tried to write a new conjecture. They worked for a while without success. The idea of using symbols like Δ + □ = ♥ seemed to help them explain what this big idea would say about this number sentence. They quickly wrote ♥ − Δ = □. I provided the "if . . . then" formal language, and they agreed that they were saying, "If Δ + □ = ♥, then ♥ − Δ = □." They then wrote the following conjecture:

if Δ + □ = ♥ then ♥ − Δ = □

They thought that this was the best way to write the conjecture and later shared the conjecture with the class.

Tara DeSciscio-Fussell, Third-grade teacher

Multiplication and Division

Multiplication and division are related in essentially the same way as addition and subtraction.

The Relation Between Multiplication and Division

- If $a \div b = c$, then $a = c \times b$
- If $d \times e = f$, then $d = f \div e$ for $e \neq 0$, and $e = f \div d$ for $d \neq 0$

As was the case with addition and subtraction, understanding the relation between multiplication and division is critical for learning division number facts and for dealing flexibly with problem situations involving multiplication and division.

OPERATING ON BOTH SIDES OF THE EQUAL SIGN

Consider how one third-grade student used relational thinking to figure out what number could be substituted for d to make the following a true number sentence:

$$345 + 576 = 342 + 574 + d$$

Sam:	There's 300 on each side, so I took them off, and you can do the same thing with the 500s. That gave me 45 plus 76 equals 42 plus 74 plus d. Now you can do the same thing again with the 40s and the 70s, and that leaves 5 plus 6 equals 2 plus 4 plus d. And that's 11 and 6, so d has to be 5 to make that side 11.
Ms. V.:	Sam, how do you know that you can do that?
Sam:	If something is the same on both sides of the equal sign, you don't even have to think about it, you can just get rid of it. When you get rid of what's the same, the numbers get smaller and then it gets real easy to tell what d is equal to.

To transform the original number sentence, Sam used a basic property of equality. First he subtracted 300 from both sides of the equation. Then he did the same thing with 500, 40, and 70. Because he subtracted the same numbers from both sides of the equation, the two sides remained equal. This property and corresponding properties for addition, multiplication, and division are given in the following list.

Operating on Both Sides of the Equal Sign

- If $a = b$, then $a + c = b + c$
- If $a = b$, then $a \times c = b \times c$
- If $a = b$, then $a - c = b - c$
- If $a = b$, then $a \div c = b \div c$ when $c \neq 0$

These properties play a central role in the solving of algebraic equations. Much like the strategy that Sam used to simplify the equation he was working with, algebra students solve equations by simplifying them using these properties. After one adds, subtracts, multiplies, or divides, each of the simplified equations has the same solution as the original equation. For example, consider the solution to the equation in Figure 9.1. The starred (*) steps involve applications of the previously listed properties. Simplifying these equations also involves a number of additional steps based on other properties. A more complete version of the solution of this equation appears in the Challenges.

a. $16y + 24 = 12y + 56$
b. $16y + 24 - 24 = 12y + 56 - 24$*
c. $16y = 12y + 32$
d. $16y - 12y = 12y + 32 - 12y$*
e. $4y = 32$
f. $\frac{1}{4} \times (4y) = \frac{1}{4} \times 32$*
g. $y = 8$

FIGURE 9.1
Operating on Both Sides of the Equal Sign to Solve an Equation

PROVING CONJECTURES ABOUT SUBTRACTION AND DIVISION

Most conjectures about subtraction or division can be proved by relating them to corresponding conjectures involving addition or multiplication. For example, consider the conjecture about subtracting a number from itself ($d - d = 0$, *for all numbers*).

We start with what we know about adding zero to a number: $d + 0 = d$. Next we use what we know about the relation between addition and subtraction (if $a + b = c$, then $c - a = b$) to rewrite the corresponding subtraction problem. In this case the d that is added to zero corresponds to a, and the d to the right of the equal sign corresponds to c. Thus, we have $d - d = 0$.

Similarly, we can prove that $p \div 1 = p$, *for all numbers*.

We could start with $p \times 1 = p$ and use a similar proof to the one we used for $d - d = 0$, but instead we use a slightly different form of the proof. Either approach is valid.

Take the $p \div 1$ as unknown: $p \div 1 = \square$. Using the relation between division and multiplication, this implies: $p = \square \times 1$. We know that when 1 is multiplied by p the result is p, and p is the only number for which $\square \times 1 = p$. Therefore, $\square = p$, and $p \div 1 = p$.

We now also can show why *we cannot divide by zero*.

Suppose we could divide by zero: $r \div 0 = \square$. Using the relation between division and multiplication, this implies $r = \square \times 0$. When zero is multiplied by any number, the result is zero. In other words, there is no number that we can multiply by zero and get r unless r is zero. This shows that we cannot divide any non-zero number by zero.

It also turns out that we cannot divide zero by zero: $0 \div 0 = \square$ would imply that $0 = \square \times 0$. Here we have an embarrassment of riches; we could substitute any number for $\square$. That also is a case that we do not want. We could choose one number as the answer when we divide zero by zero, but that leads to other problems. Therefore, we conclude that any number divided by zero is undefined.

We also can now show why *we invert and multiply when we divide fractions*.

Consider the general case $a/b \div c/d = \square$, where a/b and c/d are any fractions.

Using the relation between division and multiplication, this implies $a/b = \square \times c/d$. Now we want to solve this equation for $\square$. We can do that by multiplying both sides of the equation by d/c:

$$
\begin{aligned}
a/b \times d/c \; &= (\square \times c/d) \times d/c \\
&= \square \times (c/d \times d/c) \\
&= \square \times 1 \\
&= \square
\end{aligned}
$$

Thus, $\square = a/b \times d/c$, which shows that $a/b \div c/d = a/b \times d/c$.

INVERSES

Note that in the previous proof and in the solution of the equation earlier in this chapter, both sides of the equations were multiplied by a number that was selected so that the product of that number and the number it was multiplied by was 1. This turns out to depend on another important property.

For every number r except zero, there is a unique number $1/r$ such that $r \times 1/r = 1$. This number is called the *multiplicative inverse* or *reciprocal* of r.

The reciprocal of 7 is $1/7$, and the reciprocal of $1/7$ is 7. The reciprocal of $^3/_4$ is $^4/_3$. In general, for any fraction a/b, the reciprocal is b/a. Observe that when we invert and multiply to divide fractions, we are multiplying by the reciprocal. In other words, any division problem can be recast as a multiplication problem in which multiplication by the reciprocal of the divisor replaces division ($p \div q = p \times 1/q$). A similar property applies to addition.

> *Every number (including zero) also has an additive inverse or opposite.*
> *The opposite of any given number r is the number (–r) that gives zero*
> *when added to r.*

The opposite of 7 is –7, and the opposite of –7 is 7. The opposite of $^3/_4$ is $– {}^3/_4$. The opposite of zero is zero. As with multiplication, all subtraction problems can be recast as addition problems involving addition of the opposite of the number being subtracted [$p – q = p + (–q)$]. For example: $5 – 7 = 5 + (–7)$ and $4 – (–6) = 4 + 6$.

Replacing subtraction by adding the opposite and division by multiplying by the reciprocal provides some simplicity. With addition and multiplication, we do not have to worry about changing the order or grouping of numbers that we are adding or multiplying. For example, we cannot regroup for the following problem represented by subtraction, but we can for the equivalent representation using opposites:

$(18 – 7) – 5$ is not equal to $18 – (7 – 5)$,
but $(18 + (–7)) + (–5)$ is the same as $18 + ((–7) + (–5))$

If we only deal with addition and multiplication, we have much simpler rules for order of operations: first, combine terms in parentheses in the appropriate order, then multiply before adding.

From a purely mathematical standpoint, the fact that subtraction can be replaced by adding the opposite and division by multiplying by the reciprocal makes subtraction and division somewhat superfluous operations. But that does not mean that we will do away with them. Subtraction and division still have a place in the mathematics curriculum and in our daily lives. They are ingrained in our culture, they provide natural representations for a variety of problem situations, and they provide useful computational schemes for dealing with large numbers.

THE BASIC PROPERTIES REVISITED

We now have introduced the basic properties we need to develop most of arithmetic and algebra. Some of the properties we have discussed along the way are more critical than others, and some can be derived from other properties. In Table 9.1, we have listed the most fundamental properties upon which arithmetic and algebra are built.

Many of the properties we identified in Chapter 4 are not in Table 9.1. That is because they can be derived from these properties and as a consequence are not fundamental. Not surprisingly, all of the properties involving

TABLE 9.1
The Fundamental Properties of Number Operations

Properties of Addition	
Identity	For every real number a, $a + 0 = a$
Inverse	For every real number a, there is a real number $-a$ such that $a + (-a) = 0$
Commutative	For all real numbers a and b, $a + b = b + a$
Associative	For all real numbers a, b, and c, $(a + b) + c = a + (b + c)$
Properties of Multiplication	
Identity	For every real number a, $a \times 1 = a$
Inverse	For every real number a, $a \neq 0$, there is a real number $1/a$ such that $a \times 1/a = 1$
Commutative	For all real numbers a and b, $a \times b = b \times a$
Associative	For all real numbers a, b, and c, $(a \times b) \times c = a \times (b \times c)$
Distributive Property of Multiplication over Addition	
	For all real numbers a, b, and c, $a \times (b + c) = (a \times b) + (a \times c)$

subtraction and division are missing. The multiplication property of zero ($a \times 0 = 0$) also is not included, because it can be derived from the properties in Table 9.1 (see Challenge 6 in Chapter 8).

CHALLENGES

1. Here is an expanded version of the steps involved in solving the equation discussed in this chapter. Identify the properties that justify each of the steps.

   a. $16y + 24 = 12y + 56$
   b. $(16y + 24) - 24 = (12y + 56) - 24$
   c. $16y + (24 - 24) = 12y + (56 - 24)$
   d. $16y + 0 = 12y + 32$
   e. $16y = 12y + 32$
   f. $16y - 12y = (12y + 32) - 12y$

g. $16y - 12y = (32 + 12y) - 12y$
h. $16y - 12y = 32 + (12y - 12y)$
i. $(16 - 12)y = 32 + (12 - 12)y$
j. $4y = 32 + 0y$
k. $4y = 32 + 0$
l. $4y = 32$
m. $\frac{1}{4} \times (4y) = \frac{1}{4} \times 32$
n. $(\frac{1}{4} \times 4)y = \frac{1}{4} \times 32$
o. $1y = 8$
p. $y = 8$

2. Prove that $a - 0 = a$.
3. Explain why the opposite of the opposite of any number is the number you started with (i.e., $-(-r) = r$).
4. Prove the following: If $a \times b = 0$, then $a = 0$ or $b = 0$.
5. Use Challenge 4 to solve the following equation: $(2y - 12)(y - 5) = 0$.
6. Use the distributive property and what you learned in Challenge 5 to solve the following equation: $y^2 - 8y + 15 = 0$.
7. Use what you have learned in the preceding challenges to solve the following equation:
   $(y - 2)(y - 3) = 2$. Show how you would justify your solution.
8. The teacher in Commentary 9.1 used a story problem to help her students engage in a discussion of the relationship between addition and subtraction. Another way to initiate this discussion is with true/false number sentences. Develop a set of true/false or open number sentences that might encourage your students to make explicit the relation between addition and subtraction. What questions might you ask to help students focus on this relation?
9. Develop a set of true/false or open number sentences that might encourage your students to make explicit the relation between multiplication and division. What questions might you ask to help students focus on this relation?
10. Develop a set of true/false or open number sentences that might encourage your students to make explicit the fact that they can add or subtract the same number to the expressions on both sides of the equal sign. What questions might you ask to help students focus on this property?
11. Try the number sentences that you wrote in Challenge 8, 9, or 10 with your students. What did you learn?

CONCLUSION

For many students and adults, arithmetic represents a collection of unrelated and arbitrary manipulations of numbers and symbols, and algebra is perceived as a separate collection of meaningless procedures that are only tangentially related to arithmetic. In this book, we have portrayed a very different conception of arithmetic and algebra: one in which students learn that arithmetic and algebra are grounded in big ideas and that understanding these ideas can make arithmetic and algebra make sense.

There is a small list of fundamental numerical properties that accounts for all symbol manipulation in arithmetic and algebra. The most basic of these properties are summarized at the end of the last chapter. Developing an intuitive sense of these properties is a natural consequence of learning arithmetic with understanding, in that children who understand mathematics implicitly use fundamental numerical properties in carrying out arithmetic calculations. Although these properties may seem obvious and natural, they are very powerful. They impose a logical structure on arithmetic and algebra, and all arithmetic and algebraic operations and procedures must be consistent with them. As illustrated in the latter chapters of this book, the properties can be applied one after another to generate all valid procedures in arithmetic and algebra. Children's invented procedures for adding, subtracting, multiplying, and dividing are based on these properties, as are all computational algorithms.

We do not expect that all of the arguments shared in the previous two chapters will be understood by all children during their elementary school years, but we think it is important for all children to learn that arithmetic and algebra make sense and that arithmetic and algebra are grounded in a basic collection of big ideas. It is not sufficient, however, that children only learn the big ideas of mathematics. To understand and appreciate mathematics, they also need to understand how those ideas are used. They need to understand the practices of mathematics. In particular, they need to learn the importance of generalization; they need to learn how to represent mathematical ideas accurately using natural language and mathematical symbols; they need to learn to appreciate the value of justifying mathematical statements and to gain some insight about what is entailed in mathematical justification. Perhaps most important, students need to develop the disposition that mathematics makes sense and that they can make sense of it.

DEVELOPING MATHEMATICAL THINKING

In the preceding chapters, we have identified some of the big ideas in mathematics and how children may be engaged in learning those ideas. Two important influences on how children learn those ideas are (a) the tasks they engage in and (b) the interactions they have about those tasks.

Tasks for Learning and Expressing Mathematical Ideas

The primary context that we have discussed for developing mathematical thinking has been true/false and open number sentences. We are not suggesting that these are the only contexts for developing mathematical thinking. In fact, in *Children's Mathematics,* much of our emphasis was on using basic word problems for developing meaning for mathematical operations and procedures. Once children have a good understanding of basic operations, the next step is to reflect on important properties of those operations so that students can use their knowledge more flexibly and extend their understanding of arithmetic to algebra. That is where true/false and open number sentences come in. They provide a useful tool for focusing students' thinking on specific mathematical ideas. We have seen how number sentences could be used to

- engage students in discussions about the appropriate use of the equal sign;
- encourage students to use relational thinking;
- foster students' reliance on fundamental mathematical properties when learning number facts, place value, and other basic arithmetic concepts; and
- help students generate conjectures.

In each case, number sentences can help focus discussion and student attention. In particular, number sentences can be written to concentrate on a specific mathematical idea or misconception. For example, we saw how using a number sentence such as $35 + 97 = 97 + 35$ can encourage students to articulate a basic property about addition. We also saw how number sentences could enhance the learning of number facts by calling students' attention to a specific relation between number facts. For example, number sentences such as $9 \times 7 = 10 \times 7 - 7$ can call students' attention to the specific relation between number facts involving 9 and related number facts involving 10. At another time, this same general type of number sentence might be discussed in relation to the distributive property. Thus, this use of number sentences does not simply illustrate a trick for helping to recall number facts; it embodies basic mathematical properties.

Number sentences also can provide a window into students' mathematical thinking. Students' responses to specific number sentences can provide insight about how they are thinking about the specific ideas represented in the number sentences. Another way in which number sentences can be used to find out about students' mathematical thinking is by letting students write number sentences that they think are interesting in some way. Students often will write number sentences that do not require difficult computation because they can be simplified using a basic property of number operations. These number sentences, which are illustrated in examples in Chapter 3, both afford insight into the understanding of the student who writes the number sentences and provide artifacts that can serve as a basis for the class to discuss the properties illustrated by the number sentences.

Thus, true/false and open number sentences offer structure and possibility. You can carefully structure them to draw out a particular mathematical idea, or you can let the students generate ones that make sense to them. Students typically like arguing about true/false number sentences. They rarely hesitate to respond whether a number sentence is true or false or they are not sure, and after they answer there is opportunity for discussion that delves deeper into their thinking.

Finally, number sentences provide students a tool for representing mathematical ideas. Representing mathematical ideas using variables is one of the most important things that students learn in their mathematics education. Typically, learning to use variables to represent mathematical ideas is not addressed until students are in high school, and even then it often is neglected in favor of learning to manipulate symbols. As illustrated in Chapter 6, elementary students can learn to represent mathematical ideas symbolically, which significantly enhances their ability to communicate mathematical ideas clearly and precisely. Developing this broad conception of the use of variables also will give them a good foundation for learning algebra.

TEACHER COMMENTARY C.1

The first time I tried true/false number sentences with a group of second- and third-grade children I had been teaching, I was nervous—nervous about what students would or wouldn't say, worried that I wouldn't know how to respond. I had my number sentences written on index cards so I could put them in my pocket, pull them out at a moment's notice, and shuffle through them to find just the right one to pose next. So, I just started; the students responded. I tried to get each student to take a stand: true, false, not sure. I asked students from each response category to explain their thinking. The students explained. I posed another problem. We did it all again. I learned so much, about the number sentences, about the students' mathematical thinking, and about the development of conversation around the ideas. I was surprised by what some of my students said; I was taken aback by how adamant some could be. I couldn't wait to try it again. And I have tried it again, many times. I am still not sure that I always use the most appropriate and challenging number sentence, but I know each time I use number sentences, I get better at anticipating what students might say and what number sentence might push their thinking in productive ways.

I worry about reaching all students. At some level that worry seems like the right one to be having, but it also becomes more than a worry. I feel that I need to do something about Jay when he sits over to the side of the group not talking. I wonder what he is thinking. Or when Howard withdraws in frustration, I want a number sentence that will engage him. When India doesn't seem to want to shift toward relational thinking, I want a way to show her she can try and still honor her thinking. I worry about Clyde and Cheryle, who can't seem to figure out how to participate in the arguments around the number sentences. I want to figure out what I, and others, might be doing to keep them out of it. These worries remain, and I think about them constantly. I try to watch for them, catch them, ask the students about them, and examine my own practices to see if they may be fostering less successful forms of participation.

Number sentences provide a tool that I, as the teacher, need to take advantage of. I need to attend to the thinking of each of my students. I have to develop classroom norms that allow us to question our ideas, to have it be okay to be frustrated, on the periphery, not shifting. We need strategies for engaging and reengaging. It takes constant attention on all of our parts to develop and maintain these norms; it takes class conversations and individual conversations. It takes commitment, expectation, and skill on my part, but most of all it takes listening, getting better at knowing what to listen for, and knowing how critical it is that I listen and learn constantly.

Megan Franke, Teacher and researcher

Interactions About Mathematical Ideas

The tasks that students engage in significantly influence what they learn, but equally important are the interactions that they have about the tasks. The questions that we ask and how we respond to students' responses have important consequences for what students consider important to learn and how they perceive their roles as learners and as participants in the class. One of our goals is to use questions to focus on the important mathematical ideas that we discussed at the beginning of this chapter and throughout the earlier chapters. Two questions have proven particularly productive in this regard:

- Is that true for all numbers?
- How do you know that is always true?

Ultimately these are questions that we want students to ask themselves, and we can establish that mindset by continually asking these questions whenever it is appropriate.

Another important consideration in thinking about questioning is how we respond to students when they put forth an idea. Children often are not very articulate in expressing their ideas, and we, as teachers, often want to restate what students have said to make it clearer and accessible to more students. We also may choose to restate what students have said to focus on the important mathematical ideas or to clarify the distinctions between different arguments that students have made. This sort of revoicing can play an important role in focusing the discussion on important mathematical ideas. But there also is a danger that ideas become ours instead of the students' when we repeat or write down what we think they should have said. If our reconstructions of students' ideas are too far removed from what they actually said, they may not be able to relate our version of what they said to what they meant to say. As a consequence, our version may not make sense to them. Equally important, the students may decide that their ideas are not valued. If we want to establish a classroom community in which students think that their ideas matter and that they can make sense of mathematics, we need to be careful to communicate those perspectives to them by the questions we ask and how we respond to the ideas they express.

MATHEMATICAL THINKING FOR ALL STUDENTS

One of the defining features of learning with understanding is that knowledge is connected and integrated. Students make sense of new things they are learning by connecting them to what they already know. That is why we think it is so important to attempt to understand and build on what students already know. When students learn arithmetic with understanding, they implicitly use many of the unifying properties of number operations. Making those properties explicit can help them put structure on what they are learning and thus further their understanding.

Another defining feature of learning with understanding is that when students (or teachers) learn with understanding, their learning is generative; it serves as a basis for acquiring new knowledge. Our goal is that students learn arithmetic in a way that is generative so that their knowledge of arithmetic serves as a basis for learning algebra.

We have found that elementary children can learn to engage in algebraic reasoning. Furthermore, learning the big ideas and practices of mathematics is not just for a few mathematically gifted students. In fact, a strong case can be made that it is most critical for students at risk of failing in mathematics to engage with these ideas and practices. All students can productively engage in the kinds of mathematical activity that we have portrayed, and providing students the opportunity to focus on big ideas and practices of mathematics both opens up opportunities for student learning and provides you, as their teacher, a new perspective on what they are capable of learning.

ANSWERS FOR SELECTED CHALLENGES

CHAPTER 3

2. The goal of this challenge is not to come up with a "correct" order. In fact, there is some variability in the difficulty of different number sentences depending on students' experiences. The purpose of this challenge is to consider the factors that may make problems easier or more difficult. They include:

   a. Problems with differences of one between corresponding terms are generally easier than problems with differences greater than one.
   b. Problems that involve addition are generally easier than problems that involve subtraction.
   c. Problems in which the order of the corresponding terms is switched ($96 + 67 = 67 + p$) are generally more difficult than problems in which this is not the case.

3. This challenge extends Challenge 2. In addition to the factors identified for Challenge 2, the following might be considered:

   a. Problems in which only one of the terms is changed are generally easier than problems in which both terms are changed.
   b. Problems in which the terms are changed in the same direction (both increased or both decreased) are generally easier than problems in which terms are changed in different directions.

CHAPTER 5

6. There are no values of p that make this number sentence true. It is impossible to start with a number and add 4 and get the same sum as when starting with that same number and adding 7.

CHAPTER 6

4. An even number can be represented as $2 \times m$, where m is a whole number. An odd number can be represented as $2 \times n + 1$, where n is a whole number. Alternatively, m and n can be any integer. Some mathematics books use the terms *even* and *odd* only for whole numbers and others use these terms for all integers.

CHAPTER 7

1. When you add three odd numbers you will always get an odd number.

   In this chapter, Jamie showed that that the sum of two odd numbers is even, so if we have three odd numbers, it is the same as adding an even number and an odd number. Using the same reasoning that Jamie used, an even number has no leftovers and an odd number has one leftover. When we add an even number and an odd number, all the pairs will still pair up, and there will still be the leftover. So the sum will be odd.

2. The justification is identical to the justification for $a + b - b = a$.

CHAPTER 8

1.

  a. $35 + 48 = (3 \times 10 + 5) + (4 \times 10 + 8)$ place value

  b. $= (3 \times 10 + 4 \times 10) + (5 + 8)$ commutative and associative properties of addition

  c. $= (3 + 4) \times 10 + (5 + 8)$ distributive property

  d. $= (5 + 8) + (3 + 4) \times 10$ commutative property of addition

  e. $= 13 + (3 + 4) \times 10$ number facts

  f. $= (1 \times 10 + 3) + (3 + 4) \times 10$ place value

  g. $= (3 + 1 \times 10) + (3 + 4) \times 10$ commutative property of addition

  h. $= 3 + (1 \times 10 + (3 + 4) \times 10)$ associative property of addition

  i. $= 3 + (1 + (3 + 4)) \times 10$ distributive property

  j. $= 3 + (8 \times 10)$ number facts

  k. $= (8 \times 10) + 3$ commutative property of addition

  l. $= 83$ place value

Figure 8.6   Steps Involved in Adding Two Two-Digit Numbers

2.

a. $48 \times 37 = (40 + 8) \times 37$ place value
b. $= (40 \times 37) + (8 \times 37)$ distributive
property
c. $= (40 \times (30 + 7)) + (8 \times (30 + 7))$ place value
d. $= (40 \times 30) + (40 \times 7) + (8 \times 30) + (8 \times 7)$ distributive
property

Figure 8.8   Using the Distributive Property in Multiplying Two Two-Digit Numbers

a. $(y + 7) \times (y + 5) = y \times (y + 5) + 7 \times (y + 5)$ distributive
property
b. $= (y \times y + y \times 5) + (7 \times y + 7 \times 5)$ distributive
property
c. $= (y \times y + 5 \times y) + (7 \times y + 7 \times 5)$ commutative
property of
multiplication
d. $= y \times y + (5 \times y + 7 \times y) + 7 \times 5$ associative
property of
addition used
twice
e. $= (y \times y) + (5 + 7) \times y + (7 \times 5)$ distributive
property
f. $- (y \times y) + (12 \times y) + 35$ number fact

Figure 8.9   Discrete Steps in Multiplying Two Binomials

3.

a. $(2 \times n + 1) + (2 \times m + 1)$ associative and
$= (2 \times n + 2 \times m) + (1 + 1)$ commutative
properties of addition
b. $= (2 \times n + 2 \times m) + 2$ number fact
c. $= (2 \times n + 2 \times m) + 2 \times 1$ multiplication identity
d. $= 2 \times (n + m) + 2 \times 1$ distributive property
e. $= 2 \times ((n + m) + 1)$ distributive property
f. $(n + m) + 1$ is the sum of three whole numbers, so it is a whole
number.
g. Thus, we have 2 multiplied by a whole number, which is an even
number.

Figure 8.10   Proof That the Sum of Two Odd Numbers Is an Even Number

4. a. $(a + b) - c = a + (b - c)$ If you think in terms of whole numbers, in both cases a is being increased by b and decreased by c. This intuitive justification shows why this statement is always true. A formal justification follows.

Using the concept of additive inverses from the next chapter:

$(a + b) - c$ is the same as $(a + b) + (-c)$

Now we can apply the associative property of addition, so this is equal to:

$a + (b + (-c))$

Reversing the first step, this is the same as $a + (b - c)$.

4. b. $(a - b) + c$ is *not* equal to $a - (b + c)$. We can show this with a simple counterexample: $(8 - 3) + 2 = 5 + 2 = 7$, *but* $8 - (3 + 2) = 8 - 5 = 3$.

5. Proof that $a \times 0 = 0$.

a. $a \times 0 \quad = (a \times 0) + 0$ addition identity
b. $\qquad\quad\; = (a \times 0) + (a - a)$ $a - a = 0$
c. $\qquad\quad\; = ((a \times 0) + a) - a$ Challenge 4a
d. $\qquad\quad\; = ((a \times 0) + (a \times 1)) - a$ multiplication identity
e. $\qquad\quad\; = (a \times (0 + 1)) - a$ distributive property
f. $\qquad\quad\; = (a \times 1) - a$ addition identity
g. $\qquad\quad\; = a - a$ multiplication identity
h. $\qquad\quad\; = 0$ $a - a = 0$

7. The sum of three consecutive whole numbers is divisible by 3.

The sum of three consecutive whole numbers can be represented as:

$m + (m + 1) + (m + 2)$

Regrouping using the commutative and associative properties of addition, we get:

$(m + m + m) + (1 + 2)$

This is the same as $3 \times m + 3$ or $3 \times m + 3 \times 1$.

Because of the distributive property, we know this is the same as $3 \times (m + 1)$, which is a multiple of 3 and therefore divisible by 3.

CHAPTER 9

1. Here is an expanded version of the steps involved in solving the equation discussed in this chapter. Identify the properties that justify each of the steps.

   a. $16y + 24 = 12y + 56$

   b. $(16y + 24) - 24 = (12y + 56) - 24$ subtraction property of equality

   c. $16y + (24 - 24) = 12y + (56 - 24)$ Challenge 4a in Chapter 8

   d. $16y + 0 = 12y + 32$ property that $a - a = 0$ and calculation

   e. $16y = 12y + 32$ addition identity

   f. $16y - 12y = (12y + 32) - 12y$ subtraction property of equality

   g. $16y - 12y = (32 + 12y) - 12y$ commutative property of addition

   h. $16y - 12y = 32 + (12y - 12y)$ Challenge 4a in Chapter 8

   i. $(16 - 12)y = 32 + (12 - 12)y$ distributive property

   j. $4y = 32 + 0 \times y$ property that $a - a = 0$ and calculation

   k. $4y = 32 + 0$ multiplication property of zero

   l. $4y = 32$ additive identity

   m. $^1/_4 \times (4y) = ^1/_4 \times 32$ multiplication property of equality

   n. $(^1/_4 \times 4)y = ^1/_4 \times 32$ associative property

   o. $1 \times y = 8$ multiplicative inverse and calculation

   p. $y = 8$ multiplication identity

2. Prove that $a - 0 = a$.

   Let's say we don't know what $a - 0$ equals. Let's say $a - 0 = \square$ and see if we can show what $\square$ must be.

   $a - 0 = \square$

   $\square + 0 = a$ relation between addition and subtraction

   $\square = a$ zero property of addition

   Thus, $a - 0 = a$.

3. We would add the number $-(-r)$ to $-r$ to get zero. Therefore, $-(-r) = r$.

4. Prove the following: If $a \times b = 0$, then $a = 0$ or $b = 0$.

   If $b = 0$, we are done.

   If $b \neq 0$ then there is a number $1/b$ such that $b \times (1/b) = 1$. Let's see what happens when we use this number with our original number sentence, $a \times b = 0$.

$$a \times b = 0$$

$(a \times b) \times 1/b = 0 \times 1/b$	multiplication property of equality
$a \times (b \times 1/b) = 0 \times 1/b$	associative property of multiplication
$a \times (b \times 1/b) = 0$	zero property of multiplication
$a \times 1 = 0$	multiplicative inverse
$a = 0$	multiplicative identity

5. Use Challenge 4 to solve the following equation: $(2y - 12)(y - 5) = 0$.
   Either $2y - 12 = 0$ or $y - 5 = 0$.

   So $y = 6$ and $y = 5$. You can substitute either value into the number sentences and you will get a true number sentence.

6. Use the distributive property and what you learned in Challenge 5 to solve the following equation: $y^2 - 8y + 15 = 0$.

   $$y^2 - 8y + 15 = (y - 3)(y - 5)$$

   So $y = 3$ and $y = 5$. Again you can substitute these values into the original number sentence and you will get a true number sentence.

   Note: You can use the distributive property to show $y^2 - 8y + 15 = (y - 3)(y - 5)$.

7. Use what you have learned in the preceding challenges to solve the following equation: $(y - 2)(y - 3) = 2$.

   Zero is a special number. When the product of two numbers is anything but zero we cannot make the same general statement about one of the factors. Therefore, if we want to use the same strategy we used in Challenge 5, we have to work to change this equation so that the product of two numbers is equal to zero not 2.

$(y - 2)(y - 3) = 2$	
$y^2 - 2y - 3y + 6 = 2$	distributive property
$y^2 - 5y + 6 = 2$	distributive property
$y^2 - 5y + 6 - 2 = 2 - 2$	equality property of subtraction
$y^2 - 5y + 4 = 0$	number fact/additive inverse
$(y - 4)(y - 1) = 0$	distributive property
$y = 4$ or $y = 1$	Challenge 4

   You can substitute either of these values into the original number sentence and you will get a true number sentence.

   $$(4 - 2)(4 - 3) = 2 \times 1 = 2 \quad and \quad (1 - 2)(1 - 3) = (-1)(-2) = 2$$

INDEX

Using the CD-ROM

The CD-ROM should start playing automatically. If not, follow the instructions below.

Macintosh:
1. Place the CD-ROM in the drive
2. Double click the "START" CD icon on the desktop
3. Double click the icon that corresponds to the operating system you are using:
    a. For Mac OS 9 or earlier: Click "START OS9"
    b. For Mac OS X or later: Click "START OSX"

Note: If you have both operating systems 9 (Classic) and X, and system 9 is running when you insert the CD, the CD may start automatically. If not, follow the instructions above. It is best to play the CD using OS X if available.

Windows 98, ME, 2000, and XP:
1. Place the CD-ROM in the drive
2. Double click the "My Computer" icon on the desktop
3. Double click the "START" CD icon on your drive